trust
yourself

you have the power

by dr. tony larsen

Impact Publishers
POST OFFICE BOX 1094
SAN LUIS OBISPO, CALIFORNIA 93406

Copyright © 1979
Tony Larsen

Library of Congress Cataloging in Publication Data

Larsen, Tony, 1949-
  Trust yourself.

  1. Success. I. Title.
BF637.S8L356   158'.1   79-12837
ISBN 0-915166-18-6

Third Printing, June, 1985

Cover Design by Sharon Schnare.
Back Cover Photo by Greg Berg.

Impact ⬟ Publishers
POST OFFICE BOX 1094
SAN LUIS OBISPO, CALIFORNIA 93406

ii

MY THANKS

to my family and friends, who have helped me to learn how to
handle my world more effectively, and
to the disciplines which have increased my self understanding
and my ability to help others, including
Transactional Analysis, Gestalt Therapy, Behavior
Modification, Implosive Therapy, Assertiveness Training,
Non-Directive Counseling, Rational Emotive Therapy,
Reality Therapy, est, Human Effectiveness Training,
Buddhism, Taoism, and the ethical teachings of Jesus.

CONTENTS

trust yourself
you have the power

PUBLISHER'S NOTE

Introduction:
Your Choices About This Book

You have two of them. You can either get something out of this book. Or you can complain about how you didn't get anything out of this book.

Surprised? That's the truth. It's your choice whether or not you will handle your world more effectively. This book can't make you do it. In fact, this book can't make you do anything. Only you have the power to become what you want. And if you don't want to become a more effective person, then you won't, no matter how many self-help books you read. If you really do want to become a more effective person, then you will—whether or not you read one more word on this page. All this book can do is show you some things about yourself and invite you to improve your life. It can't do that improving for you. That's a choice and a power that only you have.

You've probably gotten into the habit of thinking that people and things can make you happy or sad, interested or bored. But they don't have the power. You do. You have the power to find even "dull" people interesting. You have the power to let yourself be bored by books that others find fascinating. You have the power to take tragedy and eventually turn it around so that it doesn't completely debilitate you. And you have the power to give up your power and let the world and everybody in it victimize you.

Yes, you have the power, but you're not always willing to admit that. It's easier to believe you're an *effect* rather than a

1

cause. Then you don't have to take responsibility for anything, not even for yourself. You can just wait around for other people to try to solve your problems for you. And when they don't, you can complain about how tough life is.

What if I told you that you're a hypocrite? Would that make you mad? Of course not. I don't have the power to *make* you mad (or happy). I don't have the power to make you interested either (or bored). If you do become angry or indignant over something you read in this book, remember that your anger or indignation comes from within you. It doesn't pop out of the pages here and attach itself to you. I'm telling you now that there is some hypocrisy in you. (There is also honesty and integrity.) And I'm going to invite you to discover other things about yourself too, both good and bad. You can discover fantastic possibilities for your life. Or choose to ignore them.

I suspect that if you read this book and honestly read yourself, you may become angry at times ("How *dare* he tell me that I'm evading responsibility for making my life work?")—but I think you'll more often laugh. And after that—well, it's up to you whether you'll grow from the insight. Neither I nor anyone else can make you grow.

If you don't want to improve your life, don't bother to read this. Oh, you can go through it and then say you found it worthless and tell that to your friends and feel self-righteous. "Oh yes, I read that book and it didn't do a thing for me." Yes, you can be "right." But what good is that? Yes, you get to "win"—but who are you winning over? Not me, certainly. You won't hurt my feelings if you don't like this book. So don't read it for me. Or to please your mother. Or to satisfy a friend. Do it for you. And if you don't intend to improve your life, then don't bother reading any further. Why waste your time trying to prove something or please someone else? Either do it for you, or don't do it.

What I want you to see is that *you have the power within you!* This book is valuable *only* for helping you come to know that. That's all!

That happens to be a lot, actually. Once you see that — and decide to use it — you'll change your life. Maybe a little. Maybe a lot. Maybe more than a lot. It's great knowing you can do that, isn't it?

To give you an idea of what to expect, a few comments about organization of the book: it is divided into five parts. Part One ("Handle Your World More Effectively Without Doing a Thing") shows you how to improve living simply by changing the way you look at life's events. You're more free than you think you are, and just knowing that will help you be happier. Part Two ("Handle Your World More Effectively by Starting to Do Things") shows you that you also have the power to get more done in your life — but you must choose to do it. Part Three will deal with emotions and how to handle them constructively.

Attitudes. Actions. Feelings. Then Part Four ("You") invites you to take a good look at yourself and realize that your little routines are more funny than they are sad. And Part Five ("Making Life the Best Possible Game") is serious fun.

At the end of the book I've included a list of "Suggestions for Further Reading" keyed to each chapter. If a particular topic seems especially interesting or helpful to you, you may want to pursue it further by checking some of these references. Most of what I have to say is drawn from the work of others. I appreciate and acknowledge their contributions to my life. You may enjoy them too.

Ready to acknowledge your power and use it to improve your life? Then read on.

Part One:
HANDLE YOUR WORLD
MORE EFFECTIVELY
WITHOUT DOING A THING

Yes, it's possible to be happier, healthier, and more free without *doing* anything in the world—without changing reality at all. It's possible to live more effectively just by changing the way you *look* at reality. You have the power within yourself to make that change and consequently have more control over your feelings and responses. And the first step toward realizing this power is to accept the fact that...

1

What Is, Is

This chapter is about reality. It is about what is. This may seem like a strange subject for a whole chapter, but the truth is, many people don't realize that what is, is.

"But I don't want it to be that way." Reality doesn't care what you want. "But I hope it will be different." Well, your hoping won't make any difference in the way things are. Your *doing* something may make a difference, but your hoping won't because reality couldn't care less what you hope for. "But it *shouldn't* be this way." Right. A lot of things are that shouldn't be. It shouldn't get so cold in the winter. People should never be mean. You should have more money. Oh yes, reality should be different from the way it is. But it isn't different. It is the way it is. And you can scold it all you want—"Listen, reality, I don't want you doing things like that anymore; it just isn't right"—but reality isn't going to care what you think or feel.

"But I've worked so hard for this. It isn't *fair* that I can't have it." That's right. "After all I've done for them, *this* is what I get in return. It isn't fair." True enough. Life isn't fair.

"Well, I just won't accept it." Fine. But whether you accept it or not, reality will go its own merry way. The sun will rise in the morning whether you want it to or not, whether you hope it will or not, whether you think it should or not, whether you think it's fair or not, whether you accept it or not.

Do you know what you accomplish by wishing reality to be

different from what it is? Try an experiment with me. Pick an object in the room you are in right now, say a table or chair, and wish it to go away. Next, hope that it will go away. (Close your eyes for a moment and then open them to see if anything has happened.)

Now, is that table still there? Did anything you said get it to go away? Did anything you thought or felt get it to go away? No, the only thing that would get it to go away would be to move it. So that's fine. You can move things that can be moved. But there is a lot in reality that can't be moved away. If someone runs into your car and smashes it, you can't change that fact. You can say, "Oh no, oh no." And you can say, "Oh, if only I hadn't driven the car on this dangerous expressway." And you can say, "Why didn't I get collision insurance?" And you can say, "Why did this have to happen to me? It isn't fair, I don't deserve this." You can say all that, but nothing you say changes the fact that your car is smashed.

If someone steals your wallet and $200, you can't change that fact. You can say, "Oh, why was I so careless as to carry that much money in my wallet?" You can say, "That dirty thief." You can say, "Where are the police when you need them?" You can say, "But I needed that money, and it'll take so long to earn that much again." And you know what? The fact still remains that you're out $200.

You know, it's one thing when someone promises to do something and then doesn't follow through, so we say, "Hey, you promised. It isn't fair of you to break your promise." But we get upset at *things*, not just people. When reality isn't nice, we get angry. We forget that reality never promised us anything. Life never said, "Don't worry, I will always be fair." You would *think* it had, to see how many people rant and rave over misfortune and shake their fists to say, "It Isn't Fair!" Of course it isn't. And once you realize that there are a lot of unfair things in reality that you can't change, then you'll have more time and less distress. You'll have more time because you won't need so much for complaining about how unfair it is, and for explaining to yourself how it *should* have been, and for wishing that it could be different. And you'll have less distress because you won't be upset so often about how things haven't turned out the way you wanted.

There are two kinds of things in life. Things you can change. And things you can't change. The things that need to be changed and can be changed, by all means go ahead and change. For the things that cannot be changed, however, you still have two alternatives: you can either waste time on them and let yourself be upset over them; or you can accept them serenely. In other words, although you can't change everything in reality, you *can* change the way you look at reality. If you want to get yourself all riled up and upset all the time, then go ahead wishing and hoping that reality wouldn't be the way it is. You can practice by wishing that the table or chair in your room weren't there, as you did a few minutes ago. If you work at it, you can get yourself into a real tizzy!

If, however, you would rather reduce the amount of upset and frustration in your life, then stop fighting reality. Stop trying to wish it away. Accept it. Even choose it. Gautama Buddha said that the root of all suffering is *desire*. People *desire* things that they don't have and then if they don't get them they're sad. People *hope* for things to happen and then if they don't happen they're disappointed. People *wish* things would be different and then because they're not they get upset. Instead of desiring or hoping or wishing for reality to be other than it is, wish for it to be as it is. Or if you can't do that, at least accept it the way it is, and you'll save yourself a lot of suffering.

You and I have gotten into the habit of thinking that what we need, in order to be happy, is for reality to be different. If I had more money, more friends, a more interesting job, a nicer home, a better spouse...if I had all these things—if reality were different—*then* I would be happy. But, you know, there are people who have more money who aren't happy. There are people who have more friends or an exciting job or a nice home or a fantastic husband or wife, who aren't any happier than you are. *And*, there are people who are poor, with few friends, people who have what you would consider a dull job, who live in decrepit housing and are not married to someone with a vivacious personality— there are people like that who are happier than you are!

Hard to believe, isn't it?

Would you be happier if you had more money? Perhaps for a while. But then you'd probably get used to your new standard of living and start wishing you had even *more!* Do you realize that there are people in this world today who wish they were as smart or as healthy as *you* are? People who would love to be as creative as you are or to have a personality as charming and exciting as yours is? It's true. There are plenty of people who would envy you. You're not happy, and there are millions who wish they had it so good. Of course, that's their problem. They have the same block you have—they wish things would be different. If we would stop *wishing* things would be better, then we wouldn't mind the way they are—at least, not nearly so much.

A friend of mine came to me recently to talk about how unhappy she was at work. "My job is really depressing me," she said. (That was her first mistake. Her job didn't have the power to *do* that to her.) "My boss," she went on, "doesn't even care about employee morale. All he cares about is how much money he can get out of us. And one more thing that really gets me: They're not fair to us regarding personal purchases or salaries—if they can get away with knocking out most of our commission over a technicality, they will."

All these *outside* people and things were supposedly "making" my friend depressed. These were realities which, by and large, could not be changed—unless she took a different job. But although the *realities* might not be susceptible to change, her way of *looking* at these realities was.

When I asked her about low employee morale, she said, "The workers aren't treated as persons." "But why expect management to treat you that way?'' I asked. ''Just think of management as a programmed computer. It'll only do what it needs to do in order to squeeze money out of sales. Think of your boss as a vending machine—you put in your work, your salary pops out, and the machine just sits there not caring about you or anybody. You don't get angry at the unfriendliness of vending machines, do you? It doesn't upset you that the coke machine doesn't say, 'Thank you and have a nice day.' If your boss is as impersonal as a vending machine, then think of him that way and don't get upset.''

''But they don't even treat us fairly.'' ''OK, then just think of management not only as money-grubbing but also unjust. Whoever told you that people would always be fair? Just think of your job as a big bingo game. Bingo games are never fair. Everyone feels, '*I* should have won. I needed the prize more than the winner did.' But you don't mind losing too much because you never expected everybody to get equal shares. Once you realize that life is a big bingo game in which some win and others lose, without much regard as to who *deserved* anything or to who *should* have had anything or to any rules of fairness—once you realize that, not just in your head but experientially, you'll save yourself both time and distress.''

You know, when people climb mountains they know the mountains may turn out to be treacherous—they know the mountains are not going to go out of their way to be nice to mountain climbers—and that doesn't bother them. When you go walking down the street you know that gravity isn't going to let up so that you can sort of glide along; and that doesn't bother you. If you expected it to let you glide along, then you'd be frustrated when it didn't. If you kept wishing it would change and saying, ''It's not fair that I have to walk with gravity,'' then you'd be angry. But you generally expect mountains and gravity to be as they are.

If we had a depression tomorrow and you lost half your money, would you still be able to live? Yes, and even live happily if you had the right attitude. Oh, you'd be depressed at first — only because you were used to something else — but eventually you'd get accustomed to the new ways. You see, most of the things we need (or *think* we have to have) to be happy, are just not very important at all. Next time someone asks you to make a contribution to a charity or a social cause, don't fool yourself into thinking it's going to completely cramp your lifestyle and make you miserable to give. "It" won't make you miserable; *you* will make yourself miserable by thinking, "Boy, what I could have done with that money." Instead, just think, "I now have 'x' amount of money left to spend as I wish."

Now, there are some things that, no matter how you look at them, are bound to *invite* suffering. Like the death of a loved one, physical injury, or loss of significant possessions. But you don't have to *let* these things cause you unspeakable misery. Some people accept the death of someone they love with a kind of serenity, a kind of quietness that speaks their gratitude for having the gift of this person's life while it was there. Tears, yes, but not just tears of sorrow — tears of gratitude also.

I lost $400 several years ago — stolen out of my room. I couldn't believe it at first, and I looked all over in vain. It was money I had planned to use for a trip from Boston to San Francisco to visit my family. I *was* depressed at first, but later I thought: What if I hadn't had that money in the first place? So instead of thinking of how much money I once had and now no longer possessed, I just thought of not having it at all, and I got to California anyway. You see, there were two ways of looking at the situation: No. 1: "Oh my God, a terrible thing has happened — what will I do!"; and No. 2: "Let's see if I can use a little ingenuity to get to California with the little money I have." The facts were the same. But view No. 1 saw them as tragic, while view No. 2 saw them as a potential adventure. View No. 1 would have spoiled the entire trip. View No. 2 made it exciting all the way.

Have you ever noticed that you can go to a party and find it boring one time, but with a different frame of mind find it exciting another time? Suppose everyone at the party is into computer technology and you aren't. And there's not much you can do about getting out of the invitation. So you're not willing to change reality, though you can change the way you view it. View No. 1 is this: "I have nothing in common with this crowd, and man, will I be bored." And you probably *will* be if you go in with that attitude. View No. 2 could be any or all of the following: a) "Gee, I don't know anything about computers, but maybe I'll learn some fascinating things just from listening"; b) "If I make sure to ask questions that would put their jargon into laypersons' terms, I'll be sure to learn a lot"; c) "It will be interesting to watch the people trying to get to know each other here in the guise of so-called 'purely intellectual' conversation"; d) "During times in the group conversation when nothing interests me, I'll start writing a fantasy story in my head, like I've always wanted to do." Nothing has to be inherently boring or tragic, or at least not as awful as we are inclined to make it.

Ever notice a group of children sitting on the sidewalk on a beautiful sunny day near a park? They may be saying, "We're so bored. There's nothing to do."

"But you could play a game of tag." "Aw, that's boring too."

"Well, how about going for a walk and looking at nature?" "Aw, what's so interesting about that?" When a group of children with everything to do holds view No. 1, it has nothing to do.

Take a look at some often dreary realities: a grey, rainy day. View No. 1 says, "Boy, what a lousy day—that sure blows all my plans." View No. 2 doesn't mope about the reality or try to wish it away, but simply accepts the reality and even chooses it: "Well, today's not a good day for the beach, but it sure would be fun to put on some old clothes and splash through puddles, or else to work on some of those home hobbies I've been wanting to get to, or even to simply listen to the rain hitting the windowpanes and watch it flood the gutters." Another reality: waiting for a bus or plane. "Oh my God, I've got three hours to kill before the plane leaves. How boring." But with view No. 2, "Gee, I've got three hours to explore the airport, read a book, stop at the gift shop, watch the planes take off, look at the different people and guess where they've been or where they're going or what they're really like, write some letters, meet some new people, or write a poem." Same reality. One view wishes the reality weren't there; the other says, "*What is, is*, and I can live with that—I can even like it."

Here's a reality that I've seen time and again viewed in different lights. Someone's spouse has an affair. For one person it's the end of the world and the end of the marriage. For another it's not considered so drastic, but is still a serious breach of faith. For another, it might be a very minor problem. Same reality. Different ways of looking at it.

Now, despite the fact that you know that what is, is, and the best way to live with what is, is to accept it, and even choose it if possible—despite the fact that you know this in your head, many times you will find yourself getting upset and resisting reality and wishing it away—crying over spilled milk, as it were. When this happens, don't deny your feelings by saying, "Oh, this is silly. I shouldn't feel this way." It's true, maybe you "shouldn't" feel this way, but you do. (What is, is—even in the emotion department.) It's OK to have irrational feelings.

But don't stop there. Second step is to see why you're angry. Your friend didn't *make* you angry. Your friend didn't start beating you up, did he/she? Perhaps your friend spent the whole evening at the party with another person instead of you. Why did you get angry? Maybe you felt jealous. Why were you jealous? Perhaps because you feel true friends should always stay by each other. Why do you feel that? Well, they *should*, that's all. No, don't stop probing. Why do you feel true friends should always stay by each other? Perhaps because you feel insecure when you don't have someone to lean on. Why does that make you feel insecure? Continue asking the questions until you discover that the real reasons for your feelings aren't "out there" someplace. You may have become conditioned to feeling certain ways, but you don't have to *stay* that way. I don't guarantee your upset emotions will just disappear through looking for their real causes, but you will at least begin to take more charge over your feelings instead of having them take charge over you.

Remember, what is, is, but there is more than one way to live with what is. You can fight it and pretend it isn't there, thinking about the "good old days" when it wasn't there or the days that might have been if reality hadn't happened the way it happened. *Or* you can accept it and say, "That's the way it is, and it's OK. I may not *like* it, but I can *live* with it."

There was a woman in my church who had a sickness that gradually paralyzed her body. That was depressing to her, but not as debilitating as it might have been. She saw friends during those last months—in fact, she enjoyed herself! She liked seeing people, playing with them, being with them. She enjoyed herself. Isn't that crazy? She was about to die and she was enjoying herself! Oh, give me that kind of craziness: to accept what is, and to enjoy!

What will you choose—to live with reality...or to continually let yourself be handled by it? The choice is yours. As usual.

2

The Lost Coin

"If there is a woman who has ten silver coins, if she should lose one, won't she take a lamp and search the house from top to bottom until she finds it? And when she has found it, she calls her friends and neighbors together. 'Come celebrate with me,' she says, 'for I have found that coin I lost'" (from the Gospel of Luke, Chapter 15, verses 8-10).

You really appreciate something once you don't have it. If that woman had never lost her silver coin, she wouldn't have had a party to celebrate that she had it. Can you imagine that woman saying, "Gee, I've had these 10 silver coins all my life, and I think I'll celebrate having them"? No, she had to lose one first. *Then* she could celebrate.

You probably don't appreciate what you have because you don't remember what it's like not to have it. Were you ever lost as a child? If you were, you probably cried and cried, and then when your parents found you, you were so grateful—you never realized how important they were before. You had to lose them first.

Just recently I thought I'd lost my pocket calendar. That little book has every appointment, date, and phone number in it that I need, and I had a sinking feeling when I checked my back pocket and it wasn't there. I was sure it had slipped out someplace where it couldn't be retrieved. When I *found* it, I was so grateful that I felt like inviting my friends over to celebrate. Only, it was 2 a.m., so I decided not to!

Almost anyone would like to have an all-expense-paid

vacation trip around the world! You or I would have so much fun! But you know, there are people who have the money for that who don't enjoy it. They don't know what it's like not to have it. You do, and I do, so consequently we would know how to be grateful. But unfortunately, you don't always know how to be grateful for what you *already* have. Did you ever think of being *alive* as a gift? "Big deal," you say. "So I'm alive." But ask people who are dying what they think of life and they'll tell you they never realized what a precious gift it was to be alive until it was taken away. And if they could have it returned they would be more grateful than the rest of us could imagine. They would live with so much more appreciation of living. Dying people have told this to the living over and over, but we never seem to get it—because we don't know what it is to lose the silver coin of life.

You have health, but you don't realize how neat it is to be healthy. You have money, but you've forgotten what it's like not to have it. You have friends, but you take friendship for granted. You are free—free from prison—but you don't know what it means to have that freedom taken away. If you could lose one of these silver coins—health, financial security, friendship, freedom—then you would realize how good you had it. And if you could find that coin again, you would invite your friends over, as did the woman in the parable, saying, "Come celebrate with me; I found that coin I lost!"

Reality wasn't any different for that woman *before* she lost the coin and *after* she found it. Before she lost it she had 10 silver coins, and after she found it she had 10 silver coins. Reality was the same, before and after. But *she* was different: she was grateful, she was appreciative, she could celebrate what she had. You don't have to change reality to be happier—you just have to know what it's like not to have a valuable "coin," and then you'll be glad you do.

I'd like to suggest an exercise for you to try if you like. My telling you to be grateful, or your telling yourself to be grateful, won't necessarily make you really *feel* grateful. But if you can *experience* what it is not to have some of the good things you have, then you will be glad indeed that you do have them.

Have you ever had a dream about something awful—like being maimed or being put into prison or dying? When you woke up you were so glad it was only a dream! If you could make yourself dream that you don't have some of the things you have, you'll find more joy in living when you wake up. Try these, for example: Go around for a day with a blindfold on, and you'll really learn to appreciate your sight. Imagine yourself dying—really experience it and write about it and talk about it as if it's actually happening—and then when you bring yourself back you'll be extra glad to be alive. Live on 50¢ a day for a while and you'll be amazed how glad you'll be to have the money you have. Stay in a closet for a few hours and you'll learn anew to appreciate the sunlight. Imagine that your closest friends are gone, or your parents, or your children, really experiencing that loss—you'll rejoice that you still have them! It's sort of like banging your head against a wall. It's not so thrilling while you're doing it, but oh boy, does it feel good when you stop!

Most of all, if you can take each experience of life as if it's something you never had before, it will be as if you found that silver coin you lost. Maybe you never realized you lost it, but you did, and now it's found, and you can have the neighbors over to celebrate life.

"I, who cannot see, find hundreds of things to interest me through mere touch. I feel the delicate symmetry of a leaf. I pass my hands lovingly about the smooth skin of a silver birch, or the rough shaggy bark of a pine...I feel the delightful, velvety texture of a flower, and discover its remarkable convolutions; and something of the miracle of nature is revealed to me. Occasionally, if I am very fortunate, I place my hand gently on a small tree and feel the happy quiver of a bird in full song...At times my heart cries out with longing to see these

things. If I can get so much pleasure from mere touch, how much more beauty must be revealed by sight. Yet, those who have eyes apparently see little. The panorama of color and action which fills the world is taken for granted...It is a great pity that, in the world of light, the gift of sight is used only as a mere convenience rather than as a means of adding fullness to life.''

Helen Keller

3

I Need, I Have to,
I Don't Have the Time

"I need." "I have to." "I don't have the time." These are three expressions that probably all of us use every day. But they are not accurate, not completely honest. They sometimes keep us from seeing the truth about ourselves and about the problems we have. *I need. I have to. I don't have the time.* By the time I'm through with this chapter, you just may decide to use those expressions about half as often as you do now.

I need. I need eight hours of sleep. After all I've been through today, I need a drink. I've got a headache—I need an aspirin. I need a cigarette. I need sex three times a week. I need time for myself. I need more money. I need you.

You don't *need* all those things. You *want* them. They're not necessary for your survival. There are very few things that you absolutely need—food, shelter, sleep. And not extravagant food, or first-class housing for shelter, or hours and hours of sleep. There is very little that you need. There is very much that you want. And it's good to know the difference between what you need and what you want. "I need 8 hours of sleep." No you don't. You won't die if you don't get 8 hours. You may be a little bleary-eyed the next morning if you get only 6, but you don't *need* more. You *want* more so that you can feel more refreshed. (Then again you may be bleary-eyed after 6 hours only because you've convinced yourself you need 8, and acting refreshed after

21

only 6 hours would make you a "liar" after all these years!)
    "I need a drink." No, you don't. You want one. You don't
need cigarettes. You don't need an aspirin for your headache.
You could wait it out. You don't need sex 3 times a week. You
don't *need* sex at all. Hard to believe, isn't it? Do you know
that there are some people in this world who go through their
whole lives without having sex? (I even know a few!)
    "I need time for myself." No you don't. You won't die if
you don't get it. "I need more money." Nope. You could live
on a lot less. You wouldn't be as comfortable, but then you
don't need to be comfortable; you *want* to be comfortable.
"But I need you." You don't need anybody. You want
people—you want their love and their friendship. But you
won't die without it. You don't need anyone in order to live.
As a matter of fact, you don't need to live. You don't even
need food, shelter, and sleep, because you could let yourself
die. Some people actually choose that, and we label it suicide.
    If you're catching the drift of all this, you'll realize I'm
saying you don't need anything. You want a whole lot of
things. But you don't need a single one.
    But I hear protests. People do need things, you say. Aren't
these valid statements: "You need education to get a job.
You need time for relaxation so you won't have a nervous
breakdown. You need at least some money to live decently.
You need friends to get you through hardships. You need
food in order to live." And I agree, all of these statements
may be true. But if you examine them closely you'll see that
these are all conditional needs. Look at the second half of
each sentence. You need education *to get a job*. But do you
need to get a job? No. So in the ultimate sense you don't need
an education either. Take another one: You need relaxation
time so you won't have a breakdown. But do you need to keep
from having a breakdown? No. It would be nice to remain
sane, but you don't need to. You need food in order to live.
But do you need to live? No. You could die, if you wanted.
Many people do. There are no *absolute* necessities in this
world. There are some things that are necessary in order for

other things to happen, but those other things—like jobs, security, love, sanity, even life itself—are not necessary. In other words, although you need some things in order to have other things, since you don't really need those other things, you don't need the first things either.

Perhaps you think I'm being extreme in saying no one needs anything. Well, in a sense I am. But it's for a reason. We have gotten used to taking so-called necessities for granted. I need this. I need that. Go up sometime and ask a millionaire how much money she needs to live. "Well, 100 thousand dollars a year at the very least. For just the bare essentials. Even without the servants there's the heating bill for the mansion and the insurance for the Mercedes Benz." Then ask someone on welfare what he absolutely needs to live. Compare. Go a step further. Ask the average person in Tanzania what he needs in order to live. Do you realize that most Tanzanians are undernourished and most of them are afflicted with at least one serious disease like malaria or hepatitis? They live that way. They expect it. Enough food and good health have not been necessities for those people. Alas, they're luxury items.

Think of all the things we supposedly need today that were luxuries a generation ago. Almost everybody "needs" a refrigerator, right? Can you imagine going to the store all the time to get fresh vegetables because you have no place to keep them cold? And what would you do with meat? There's no way you could get by without a refrigerator. Or a telephone. Or electricity. But people did before. For almost a million years, as a matter of fact. And many, many do even today.

Imagine what they'll say about us in another century or two. "You mean people couldn't plan outings without being sure of the weather because it wasn't controlled? And when you called on the telephone (they didn't even use visaphones with holographic images)—when you called on the phone you might not reach your party because people didn't have portable phones to carry with them? And instead of instant transport it sometimes took people hours to get where they wanted to go. And people actually *died*? So young too. Some died at 75. How dreadful. Those poor, deprived people. How could they live like that?"

One person's luxury is another person's so-called necessity. One generation's want is another generation's need. But there are no needs, no necessities. *Everything* is a luxury item.

Look at how we distinguish between levels of want, however. If you want something very badly, you say you need it. "I need a new suit." If you want something modestly, you simply say, "I want this." If you want something but only sort of—if it's not very important to you—you say, "I would like this."

"I would like to go to Mars." I really would. Ever since I was a kid I thought it would be a neat idea to be an astronaut. Do I *want* to go to Mars? Well, the possibility of getting there is pretty remote, so I don't use the word "want." I just say I would like to go to Mars—sort of. If I said, "I *need* to go to Mars," I'd be put away. Generally speaking, then we use three different expressions to refer to three levels of want: I would like, I want, I need. "I would like an ice cream cone." (That's a very small desire.) "I want an ice cream cone." (That's an average desire.) "I need an ice cream cone." (That means I'll "just die" if I don't get one.)

Speaking of ice cream cones, remember how, when you were young, an ice cream treat took care of scrapes and bruises and tears? How little you needed then. When you grew up you needed independence, your own car, your own home, your own money. Maybe now you need prestige, recognition, success, certain friends, a particular standard of living. Perhaps you need for your children to turn out a certain way. And when you're older, when you retire, it may be amazing how little you need again. A smaller place, less money, less control over people's lives.

Why do we say "I need" when what we mean is "I want"? The answer is simple. People say "I need" because it sounds

more legitimate. "I need ten hours of sleep every night."
"You're kidding." "No, it's true. I really need ten hours of
sleep." Imagine people's reaction if you said, "I need about
five hours of sleep but I sleep twice that long because I want
to." "Do you mean to tell me you spend 5 extra hours
sleeping when you could be using that time to improve the
world? Oh my God, how selfish!"

When you go in to see your boss you normally say, "I'm
asking for a raise because I absolutely need it." Imagine
saying, "I don't need a raise in pay, I just want one."

Think about it. You say you need ten hours of sleep
because it wouldn't sound legitimate to be sleeping that long
just because you want to. You say you need more money in
your job because it wouldn't sound legitimate to say you just
want it. People have told you all your life that you shouldn't
want too much. So you've learned to say "I need this."

"I want more time for myself." "Well, you shouldn't want
so much— you have enough time already." "But I *need* more
time for myself." "Oh, well, that's different then."

"I want a new wardrobe." "Boy, are you self-centered."
"But I absolutely need a new wardrobe." "Oh, well, if you
need it, you should buy it." People don't want to let you just
want things. So you need things, and then it's OK. Oh yes,
it's very handy to call your wants needs. Then you don't have
to take responsibility for them. "So, through drunken driving
you've caused this accident." "But Officer, I love people. I
wouldn't hurt anybody. It's just that I needed a drink. You
see, I have this need. The need caused the accident, not me."

That's what rapists say. "I couldn't control myself. I just
felt this overwhelming need." No responsibility. "This
need"—this "thing" out there that isn't really you—comes
in, ties you up in chains, and drags you, its unwilling slave,
into some terrible deed. "The need came and I was powerless
to fight against it." (This is the modern way of saying "The
devil made me do it.") And it has society's sanction. I recall a
decision handed down by a judge in Madison, Wisconsin a
few years ago, concerning a young man who raped a

16-year-old girl: "Well, the girl was dressed provocatively. It wasn't the boy's fault. After all, boys that age have sexual needs (!)."

Sure, call your wants *needs* and you can cop out. You have no control over your needs, right? "I couldn't help myself. I had this need." Nonsense. You had this want. Be honest about it. It's OK to admit your wants. Don't call them needs as if you have no control over them. Just accept them as wants. You can want whatever you want to want. I give you permission. You don't need my permission or anyone else's, but I'll give it anyway in case you think you do. It's OK to want a million dollars or 3 lovers or more children or less children. I'm not saying to *act out* every desire you have, but it's OK to want things. It's legitimate. We all do.

OK, now that you can admit that you often pretend to need things when you really just want them, I want to help you expand your opportunitites, your horizons. If you go through life thinking you have all these needs, and wondering, gee, what can you do about them, you'll have very little space left to see alternatives. Look at the father who spends countless hours at his job because his family "needs" to live decently and his kids "need" a top-notch college education. His family doesn't need the money. They may want it—and then again they may not. And even if they do want it, given the choice of more money or more father, they may prefer more father. But this man will never even ask the right question as long as he thinks in terms of needs. After all, needs are "necessities"—they're the things you can't do without, can't change, right? Once he realizes that there are no such things as needs—that he doesn't need a time-consuming job because he doesn't need the money to give to his family who don't need to live according to a particular standard or need to go to certain schools—once he realizes that these are wants, which can be fulfilled or not fulfilled and aren't fixed certainties, then he can look at alternatives. Maybe making a lot of money isn't as important a want as some other things. His horizons are broadened because he now realizes there are no fixed certainties. There never were. He only thought there were.

Look at your own life. How many of your so-called needs are blocking you from trying something new, something different? You may be less trapped than you think you are. "I would love to travel, but I can't because I need the money to pay for the new furniture we're ordering." Change that to: "I want to travel. I also want (not need) new furniture." Which want is greater? Now that you see you simply have two different wants, you have a choice. If one is a need, you have no choice.

"I would love to play more tennis but I can't because my family needs me." Change that to: "I want to play more tennis. Also, my family wants me home—they don't need me there, they want me there." Now you have a choice. You always did; you just didn't know it before.

Of course, everything I've said about the expression "I need" applies equally to the expression "*I have to.*" "I need" usually refers to a person or thing. ("I need this. I need you.") "I have to" normally refers to an activity. ("I have to do this." "I have to go now.") But they are essentially interchangeable (have to = need to; need = have to have) and they are both ways of covering up wants and making them look like uncontrollable necessities. You say, "I have to go" when you mean "I want to go." "Well, I have to go now because there are things I have to do." Nonsense. You don't have to go and there's nothing you have to do. You won't die if you don't go and you won't die if you don't do those things. You just say it that way because it sounds more legitimate. Instead of saying, "Well, I have to hang up now, Mary; I've got things I just have to do"—you might try saying, "I'm going to hang up now, Mary; there are some other things I want to do." It's a little more honest. It's a little scarier because now you don't have Necessity calling you away. Mary might realize that you want to do other things more than talk to her. No necessity. All you have is your want, and that doesn't seem legitimate enough. "But I can't just say 'I want to go,'" you protest. "I have to say 'I have to go' or else I'd have to explain why I'm going." No. You don't have to go. And you don't have to *say* you have to go. You don't have to explain anything. You can go, if you want. You can say or not say whatever you want. But you don't have to say or do anything.

"I can't have fun because I have to earn 'x' amount of money." You don't have to earn that amount of money. That's a choice you made and continue to make. It's within your power to change—if you want to.

We all realize this instinctively when we watch a suspenseful movie with a psychopathic killer in it who at the end says, "But don't you see, Mildred? I had to kill all those people. And now I have to kill you too. There's no other way out. You understand, don't you?" And we groan and sigh and nod our heads because we know he's crazy. He doesn't have to kill people. But in truth, there is nothing at all that he *or* we have to do. *We're* a little crazy for thinking there is.

One last expression that keeps us from exploring alternatives and opportunities is this one: "*I don't have the time.*" Oh, we throw that one out to people—and even to ourselves—to effectively wipe out one new vista after another. You do have the time. You have all the time there is to do the things you most want to do. All you have to do is take the time away from doing the things you don't want to do. "I don't have one free hour in the day to do the painting I'd like to do." Yes you do. You could go to bed an hour later. "But I need my sleep." No, you want your sleep. "But if I don't get enough sleep I won't be wide awake." Fine. Then you want to be wide awake more than you want to paint. (Right?) There's all the time there is to do the things you most want to do. Apparently you don't want to paint as much as you want to do certain other things, like be wide awake—which is fine, if you'll just admit it.

"I wanted to help but I didn't have the time." Not true. you had the time but you wanted to do other things more than you wanted to help.

"I want to be with my family more but I don't have the time." You do have the time. You just want to spend more time on your job or whatever else, for all the benefits it will bring, than you want to spend with your family. "I don't have the time" is just another cop-out expression. It lets you pretend that Time is some terrible slavemaster who ties you up and drags you away to do things utterly against your will. But time is there for you to use as you wish, as you want. It isn't forcing you to do anything. When we say, "I don't have the time," we really mean, "I'm doing other things that are more important to me and I don't want to take time away from those things to do this thing." That's what we really mean.

I need. I have to. I don't have the time. Use these expressions, but remember that they're not literally true. You may decide to still use them sometimes because not everyone else is used to dealing with their wants and you may not want to freak people out right away by admitting yours. Also, you may not want to offend people. "I don't have the time" sounds better than "I've got other more important things to do," although it means the same thing. When you do choose to use these expressions, know what you really mean. But you just may decide to use them about half as often as you do now.

Remember, there is very little that you absolutely need. And even the little that you "need," you don't really *need*. There is very little that you have to do. And even the little that you "have to" do, you don't really *have to* do. There is no lack of "time" to do the things you most want to do; there's only lack of *clarity* about what you want to do. Once you realize that you have no needs, no have-to's, and all the time there is, you'll have plenty of free, uncluttered, open space in which to make decisions, try new experiences, and embark on exciting adventures. And you'll be free to take personal responsibility for your decisions and actions. What a glorious way to be!

4

I Can't, But

There are two more common expressions we use to close off opportunities in our lives: "I can't," and "but."

I can't. "I can't do what I want to do." Well, if what you want to do is fly to Mars or be the president of the United States or spend a million dollars, then you're probably right—you can't do those things. You also can't change your age or your past or your genetic inheritance. There *are* a lot of things you can't do. But there are also a lot of things that you can do but have been pretending you can't. "I can't see you tonight." Oh, is someone handcuffing you to your bed so that you can't get out of the house? "Well, no, but I just don't have the time to see you tonight." But you're wrong. You have all of tonight in which to see me tonight. You have all the time there is, to do what is most important to you. "But I have to do cleaning." Oh, is someone threatening to kill you if you don't clean your house? "No, but if I don't it'll be dirty and I just need a clean house." You need a clean house—you mean you'll die if it isn't clean? "Well, no, but I like it clean." Fine. Then you *want* to not see me tonight. You want, rather, to clean your house (not necessarily for the fun of cleaning, but for the results a clean house brings you). You *can* see me tonight—it's not beyond your ability or power—but you *want* to do something else. And that's okay!

"I don't want to go on deceiving her, but I just can't admit I've been lying all this time." Oh yes you can. "But she'd hate me if she knew the truth." That may be true, and you're saying that you don't want that. So it's not a question of not

31

being *able* to admit the truth. You can admit the truth, but
you don't want to do that because you think she would hate
you. Now that you've admitted you can do it, you can choose
between your two wants—your want to be honest and your
want to have her like you.

We all intuitively realize how silly it is to say we can't do
this or that when we watch a melodrama in which two
clandestine lovers desperately say to each other, "But we
can't go on seeing each other like this." And then they do—
through the whole movie!

Oh yes, we can do all sorts of things we can't do...when we
want to.

"I can't help you now." Oh yes you can. "I can't live
without him." Oh really? "I can't say what I really feel."
Why not? "Because I'd get nervous." So. You can say what
you feel and be nervous while you're saying it. A lot of people
say things while they're nervous. And not many have died as
a result.

And here's one you hear a lot these days: "I just can't be
any different from the way I am." Oh, are you made of
concrete? No, you're not. Be honest. You could be different.
You don't want to be different. That's OK. You don't have to
change just because you *can* change. You neither have to
change nor have to not change. You see, "can't" is really the
reverse of "have to." "I have to" means "I can do only
this." "I can't" means "I can only do something other than
this." "Can't" is "have to" with a negative sign in front of
it. So everything I've said about "have to" applies to the
word "can't" when it's used in the way I've talked about
here.

Confused? Stay with me—I think it'll get clearer as we go
along.

Make no mistake about it. There *are* things you can't do, but not nearly as many as you've been telling yourself. The pay-off in thinking you can't do things is that then you don't have to make hard decisions, such as between wanting to finally tell the truth and wanting no one to know the truth. You'd rather pretend there isn't any decision to make. The price you pay in thinking you can't do things, however, is that you never realize how much of life is open to you; you don't see the opportunities—you just see the restrictions, the "can'ts." So the pay-off is that you don't *have* to make decisions. The cost is that you don't *get to* make decisions. Let me say that again. The pay-off in saying "can't" is that you don't *have to* be free. The price you pay is that you don't *get to* be free.

But. Another expression that can keep you from seeing clearly and create problems for your life. "I want to ask for a raise in pay, but I'm afraid to." "I love my spouse, but sometimes he or she drives me crazy." "I want to spend more time with my children but my time is taken up with other important things." The problem with the word "but" is that it makes two sides of a sentence look as if they contradict one another, so that you can't have one side and have the other at the same time. "I want to ask for a raise *but* I'm afraid." The "but" in that sentence makes it look as if asking for a raise and being afraid oppose each other—as if you can't ask for a riase if you're afraid. "I love my spouse, but sometimes he or she drives me crazy." Again, the "but" seems to make the two ideas contradictory. The "but" gives you a problem: "I love my spouse but he sometimes drives me crazy. But I love him. But he drives me crazy. But I love him. Oh, how can that be?" You begin to sound like a commercial: "It's a candy mint. But it's a breath mint. No, it's a candy mint. But it's a breath mint. But, oh no, it's a candy mint."

Stop! You're both right. You can love your spouse *and* still

feel that she or he drives you crazy. Neither side contradicts
the other. You can also want to ask for a raise and be afraid
to. No big problem. I want a raise and I'm afraid to ask for
one. So, either you go ahead and ask for it while shaking in
your boots — other people have done that, you know. Or, you
don't ask for the raise while still wanting it. There are many
other people who want things and don't get them too. I want
a thousand dollars and I'm not going to get it. I want success,
prestige, and I don't have them. That's OK. Now, if you want
to give yourself a problem so that you can while away your
time with something, start inserting "but." "I want a
thousand dollars, but I'm not going to get it. But I want it.
But I'm not going to get it." "I want success, but I don't have
it. But I want it. But I don't have it. But I want it." Fine, if
you have nothing better to do with your time, then go ahead
and mull over all these "problems." If you've got other
important things to do, however, then change your *buts* to
ands and save yourself some time. With a *but* you seem to
have things that resist each other: "I love, but I'm afraid";
"I want this, but I want that too." With an *and* you have
things that can coexist: "I love *and* I'm afraid"; "I want this,
and I want that too." No big deal. It's OK to want completely
different things. It's OK to want things you can't have. It's
OK to feel different feelings.

All these things can coexist. Save yourself some time. Save
yourself some "heavy, heavy" pondering and cogitating.
With more *ands* and less *buts*, life may be a lot lighter than
you think. And you may just open up some new possible
alternatives for yourself!

I will be talking in Part Two about two more expressions
that we use to fool ourselves into thinking we are trapped (I'll
try" and "I hope" — see Chapter 8). Right now I'd like you to
think about something else that you've probably been
allowing to have *you*, rather than *you* having *it*. And that
something is

5

Money

Money isn't worth anything. That is, money in itself has no worth. It is *your* agreement that you will use if for trading purposes that gives it whatever value it has. Your agreement and everybody else's. If tomorrow you and a bunch of other people decided you weren't going to accept money anymore, suddenly money would lose some of its value. If *everybody* decided that, it would lose all of its value. And the only thing giving it the value it has today is everybody's deciding to accept it. When you buy something with a dollar bill, it isn't the dollar bill that is paying for it: it's your promise that if someone gives *you* one of those green pieces of paper you'll give something back—some work, a product, or whatever—and the same promise from the person you're buying from, and the promise from everyone else. Money is merely a symbol of everyone's promise. It has nothing else to back it up. There isn't gold or silver somewhere to give it value. It is completely irrelevant whether we have a place like Fort Knox to keep gold or diamonds. (Besides, even if it *were* relevant, gold and diamonds have worth *only* because people decided *they* did.) Money works because—and only because—people think it works. It has value only because people give it value. There is nothing to guarantee its being accepted other than everybody's guarantee to accept it.

Before money was invented people used to just trade things. If you had extra apples and I had extra oranges, we could give each other an amount that we thought equal in worth. But suppose you wanted to trade your apples and I wanted to trade my oranges, but I didn't want your apples and you didn't want my oranges. Then we would have a problem. And that's where the convenience of some kind of money comes in. Suppose we both had something that wouldn't spoil, and yet was still considered valuable, say, pretty rocks. Well, we could trade with those and then use them later to trade with someone else who did want our oranges and apples. Historically there have been many things people used like that: cattle, leather, furs, olive oil, booze, slaves, copper, gold, silver, wampum beads, and cigarettes—all were money. All of those things happen to have been useful and valuable in themselves, and that's why they started out as a medium of trade. But that wasn't really important. What was important was that people agreed they were valuable.

Until just a few years ago our dollar bills said that they were redeemable as lawful money at the U.S. Treasury or at any Federal Reserve bank. They don't say that anymore. Because they already are lawful money. There is no gold or silver to back them up. They aren't worth anything in themselves. But we all agree to have them be worth something and so they are (even if rapidly shrinking!).

We've come a long way. From trading with things like cattle and lamp oil that we agreed were valuable because we could use them—to things like pieces of weird paper that we agree are valuable because everyone agrees they're valuable.

So now we know that money in itself has no power or value. It's your agreement, and other people's agreement, that gives it value. (And you probably thought *you* had value only if you had a lot of that green paper, when the truth is that the green paper has value only because you and everyone else decided to give it value!)

A few other important things to remember about money. If there's too much around, it goes down in value. If tomorrow the government gave out twice as much money as we now have, then everybody would have more to spend. But there would still be the same amount of things to buy, and with everybody competing for them, the sellers would raise their prices. So, the more the money, the more it takes to buy things, and thus the less its value. Actually, you also reduce the worth of money by just encouraging people to buy on credit, because then they can spend more than they have and bid up prices. Also, when people put their money in banks, the banks don't keep it there—they loan it out. So even when you save your money instead of spending it—you're really just giving it to other people to spend. And the more money there is for someone to spend, the higher the prices go. (Although if the loaned money is used to make things, then there are more products to buy, which lowers prices.)

On the other hand, the higher the prices go, the more the sellers will earn and thus the sellers will be encouraged to make more products so they can get it. And more products will mean they'll have to lower their prices in order to compete for your money. Besides, they will need more people to help make the products, so they'll create more jobs. But with more jobs, more people will have money to spend, and with more money to spend the prices will go up and people will complain. On the other hand, if people don't have jobs, they'll have to go on welfare, and if they get good welfare payments, then they have money to spend. But they're not producing anything for anyone else to buy, so there's more money going around for people to spend but only the same amount of products to buy, and the competition for the products bids up the prices.

There are at least three ways to lower the prices of things. One way is to take people's money away so they don't have that much to spend, and sellers will have to lower their prices to get the little they can. You could do this by raising taxes. You wouldn't be very popular, however, because although people would like to pay less, what good is it if they have less to pay with?

Another way to lower costs is to get more products made with the same amount of work hours. With more things to buy, there would be more competition to get people's money and prices would go down. One way to accomplish this is to get workers to work faster and harder so they can produce more. But then, of course, they'd probably want more money and if they got it, up would go the prices again! So the best way to accomplish this feat is to invent some way to produce more, more cheaply. (But if you put people out of work thereby, they will be unhappy and unable to take advantage of the lower prices because they won't have much money—or if they do get much money from welfare payments, then they'll be able to bid up prices and undo the advantage to society of your invention). The system really is complex!

Another way to increase products and thus lower prices is to stop war. You see, the defense industry gives people jobs and money, but the workers aren't producing anything for others to buy, so there's more money and less products, with higher prices as a result. On the other hand, a lot of people wouldn't feel very secure with*out* a defense system. The purpose of defense is to scare the other people into not attacking you. If you could just get everybody to agree not to hurt each other, then you wouldn't need to make bombs that sit and become obsolete. You could have people make civilian goods instead, thus increasing the number of things to buy and lowering their prices. The ironic thing is that humans all pretty much agree to give value to money. But we *don't* agree to not hurt each other. If people would just agree to love each other more, they'd save money! And enjoy life a lot more, too!

Ah, but we can't get enough people to agree to that. So we have armies and police and guns and bombs—and higher prices. But we do agree to give value to money. And it is that agreement that gives it its value. Money doesn't give value to people. People give value to money. And if you really understand that, you're ready to hear about *having* money rather than *being had by* money.

There are actually four ways of relating to money. You can have it and be had by it. You can have it and not be had by it. You can not have it and yet still be had by it. And you can not have it and not be had by it either.

In other words, you can be rich and, despite your freedom from normal financial worries, still be obsessed with money. You can be rich and not be obsessed. You can be poor and still be possessed by the desire to get it. And you can be poor and not mind at all.

A common error among some people who live frugally or even ascetically, is that they think they are free from materialistic pursuits. But you see, if you're always trying to live frugally, then you are constantly preoccupied with money. Everything you have and do is controlled by cost. What determines value for you is then the lowness of cost rather than the highness of it. But it's still cost. Unlike those who have it and are had by it, you don't *have* it—but you're *had by* it just the same. The Buddha learned this lesson as a young man when he left his rich palace in order to live ascetically so that he could "subdue" the flesh. After trying asceticism for a while, he realized that if he had to fight the desires of the flesh all the time, he was still being a slave to them. So he developed his philosophy, called the Middle Path of Buddhism. Middle, meaning in between the pursuit of hedonism and the pursuit of poverty. Either pursuit is still a pursuit. Either extreme is still an attachment. The Middle Way is to not be a slave to either.

There's a Buddhist story that illustrates the point rather well: Two monks came across a wide puddle that blocked the path of a beautiful woman. One monk carried her across. An hour later his companion reminded him that monks weren't supposed to have anything to do with women. The first monk replied, "I put her down an hour ago. Apparently you've been carrying her for miles."

If you've been carrying the burden of attachment to money all these miles, I want to talk to you about lightening that burden. I'm not going to tell you to try not to be controlled by money, because if you're always having to try *not* to be controlled, then you're in its grip just as tightly as the person who is more obviously controlled. All I want to do is show you that *you* are the one who gives money its power. If you want to let money have power over you, that's your choice — but I want you to know that you have the *power* to give up your power...or to keep it!

I want you to look at the things your money buys. Suppose you want a refrigerator. Now you could buy a new one for $500. Or you could buy an old one for $20. The difference will be that the $500 one will look nicer, last longer, and have more convenience features. But they'll both keep things cold, which is what refrigerators are for. In other words, you pay $20 for the refrigeration and $480 for looks and a frost-free mechanism. Are the looks and conveniences really worth $480? Well, people buy new refrigerators all the time, so they're worth it to them. But just because other people say something is worth so much — doesn't mean you have to agree. You are the one who decides what something is worth *to you*. You don't have to let others decide that for you.

Take a fancy new car. The basic thing a car gives you is transportation. Now, you can buy one for $500 or less that will get you around and probably last a few years. Or you can buy one for $5,000 that will look better and last a little longer and maybe get better mileage. Is all that worth the extra 4 or 5 thousand dollars to you? *Some* people say they're buying a new car only so that they can save money on repair bills and gas. They're usually fooling themselves. They should make a list comparing costs. How much more will you really have to pay for repair bills on an older car? Remember that even new cars sometimes go haywire, and anyway, after a few years your new car will probably need just as many repairs as an older one. Remember also how fast your new car depreciates within the next few years. And don't forget that collision insurance is higher for later models and that if you're making car payments, then you'll end up paying for more than the purchase price. Then compare that with what you'll save on gas and repairs. If your only purpose is to save money, getting a brand new car is probably not going to do that for you. Be honest about it. If you're buying a new car it's mostly because you like new things—they look and feel better to you. Don't pretend that you're being thrifty. Even the increasing prices of gas and oil have only a small—although increasing—effect on this decision.

You know, I see this sort of thing happen all the time. People don't want to admit their real reasons for wanting things. "God forbid that anyone would think I'm being materialistic. Oh no, it's because I'm so *un*materialistic that I'm buying this Mercedes Benz. Just think of the money I'll save in the long run." Yep. A friend of mine had a Mercedes. It was built so well that whenever something went wrong he had to pay twice as much to get it fixed because the parts are so good, they cost more. Yeah, it'll save you money...in the long run...if you don't mind waiting a hundred years for the long run to arrive.

How about a vacation trip to Hawaii? I can get tan at the local beach and go to the night spots here without spending hundreds of dollars to do it somewhere else. Another person might find a Hawaiian vacation infinitely more valuable than the cost. The important thing is that *you* decide what worth *you* will give to things, instead of believing that they can't be fun unless they cost plenty.

I'm not telling anyone not to buy a new car or refrigerator, by the way. And I'm not telling you to forget about Hawaii or to buy your clothes at Goodwill. I'm just telling you to be honest with yourself about why you want what you want. Decide what is worthwhile to *you*. You're the one who gives worth to things. Not Madison Avenue. Not the Joneses. You. You have the power to give value. Just acknowledge that.

And if you do, then you'll find that money won't control you so much anymore. Look around you at the cost of things. Take salt, for instance. I have a box of salt that contains about a pound and a half. It'll probably last me 20 years. It cost 20 cents. A penny a year. I would be willing to pay much, much more for that. If you have a son in high school you know that a boy can spend $100 or more on the senior prom, what with the corsage and tuxedo rental and dinner, etc. And why is it worth it? Because everybody else says it is and he believes them.

Another example of the relativity of cost and values: I live in an apartment, and my electric bill is usually five to ten dollars a month. I would be willing to pay fifty or even a hundred dollars for the convenience of electricity. It's important to *me*.

Consider the cost of communicating to someone across country. For not much more than a quarter I can write a letter, make a phone call, or send a tape with my voice on it to family and friends who live 2,000 miles away. That's worth a lot more to me than 25¢. On the other hand, it costs almost as much to talk on the phone to someone in a city 30 miles away as it does to call 2,000 miles away. The value of that is much less to me. Look around and see what you pay for things. I'm sure you'll find, as I did, that you pay a lot less for some things than they're worth to you, and you pay a lot more for some things than the value they give. Rejoice for the things that cost less than what they're worth to you. And stop buying the things that aren't worth what you pay!

Life has plenty of freebees around, you know. Some of them may be more valuable to you than the things you're shelling out your hard-earned cash for. Instead of giving your friend a sweater for Christmas, for example, you could give a poem you wrote that expresses your good feelings about that person. Instead of a tie you could send a warm-fuzzy letter. (See Chapter 15.) Instead of going out to an expensive dinner with your spouse or friend, you could have chicken at home under candlelight. Instead of going to a movie, you could get your friends together, all start out with the same beginning sentence, and then each write your own story. After 20 minutes read and compare...and enjoy. You can take a walk on the beach and pretend you're on a desert island. You can hug your friend for a long time. You can put on your swim suit and dance in the rain. You can walk down the street pretending that each person you see is from outer space and then try to guess what their home planet is like. And you can just sit and talk with friends as you gulp down apple juice and popcorn.

I'm not telling you to choose any one of these over more costly activities. I'm just telling you that you do have a choice. No one can tell you what anything is worth to you. Only you have the power to do that.

In case you think I'm putting down money, by the way, you've got me wrong. Money is simply people's agreement to trade and give value to things. It is neither the root of all evil nor the source of all good. It simply is. And there's no getting around it, because even trying to live without it ends up with being controlled by it. I am not even against materialism so much as I'm against your not acknowledging that *you* are the source of value. Not things. Not social pressure. Not status. You. I'm against you not acknowledging your own power. And if you *are* abdicating that power, then that's not really as immoral...as it is sad. It's a pity that you refuse to be free.

Acknowledge it: Not only do people give money its value, they also give each thing that money buys its value. You are the power behind it all. It's not out there. It's in you. Know that. Choose that. And be free.

Part Two:
HANDLE YOUR WORLD
MORE EFFECTIVELY
BY STARTING TO
DO THINGS

Now that you've seen how you can be happier by just changing the way you look at reality (your attitude), I want to show you how to improve your life by changing reality itself (that is, by *doing* things to reality, by action).

Each part of this book can stand alone. You can get something out of what follows, on getting things done, without taking a single bit of advice from what I've said in Part One. You could even start believing that outside people and things have the power to make you happy or sad. You could do all that and *still* come out ahead by reading Part Two, because Part Two shows you how to start doing things. And even if you don't believe you have any power over your attitudes or feelings, you still have the power to choose to do those things that you believe will "make" you happy and "make" you have the right attitude.

Naturally, Part Two works best in tandem with the rest of this book. It's up to you whether you will get the maximum effect through combination, or a lesser effect through taking it alone.

So make that choice. And read on.

6

What Do You Want?

One of the first things it would be good for you to know before you start getting ready to do things is this: What do you want? This is by no means an easy thing to discover, partly because wants change over time, partly because there isn't really any good reason for why you want what you want, and partly because "want" is such a vague word. You use it so often, you've probably never thought much about what a want actually is. I'd like you to think about that now. To help you do this I'm going to suggest some avenues of analysis.

First of all, as I discussed in Chapter 3, we generally use three different expressions for wanting: "I would like" (which means "I sort of want" or "I want a little"); "I want" (which means "I moderately want"); and "I need" (which isn't literally true but means "I want very, very much"). In other words, there are different degrees of wanting.

So far, pretty simple. Now, has anyone ever said to you: "Make up your mind. Do you want to or not? It's as simple as that." And maybe you felt confused because you felt that somehow it wasn't that simple. It *is* possible to want something and not want it at the same time. That's right. Sometimes we have conflicting wants. I want to go out tonight and I also don't want to because I'd like to work at home. That's a relatively simple case of conflicting desires. All you have to do is decide which want is greater and then choose it. One way to see which one is greater is to look at whether you feel comfortable using the expression "I need,"

"I want," or just "I would like." Those three expressions give you a general sense of degree, arranged as they are in descending order of preference. If you can't tell which of your wants is greater, because they're both about equal, you still choose one anyway.

Now, some smooth talkers will try to make you sound like a liar by implying that you can't want two conflicting things. (They usually do this to manipulate you.) Look at the following conversation:

Other: "Do you want to go with me?"
You: "Sure, but I've got some work to do."
Other: "Then you *don't* want to go with me."
You: "No, I do, it's just that this work is important."
Other: "Listen, you either want to go with me or you don't."

If you're easily manipulated, you might feel guilty and end up going with the person. But what was the truth about this situation? The truth was that you wanted to go with the person and you also wanted to *not* go with the person (because you wanted to do work instead). But one want was greater than the other—namely, your desire to work. (You can tell this by substituting "need," "want," or "would like" into the sentence. "I would like to go with you but I need to do work" would probably feel comfortable. Which means that the want to work is considerably greater than the want to go out. Remember, though, that the need is not *really* a need—it's just a strong want, as I've explained in Chapter 3.)

Hang in there, it gets worse before it gets better!

There's still another distinction to make here. The work you want to do may be a task that you don't really want to do (because it's difficult, for example). In this case it's not that you would enjoy working more than you would enjoy going out. No, *now* we're talking about a difference in *kind*, not just in degree. One kind of want is a desire for something *in itself*. The other kind of want is a desire for something *only* for what it will get you. For example, I may want money, but in order to earn it I have to do unpleasant work. So in one sense I don't want to work, because I don't like unpleasant tasks. In another sense I do want to work because I want the money it will get me. Actually, even the money that I want, I want not for itself but for what it will get me—for example, food and shelter. And even the food and shelter I want not for themselves but for what they give me—life and comfort. Actually, many, if not most, of the things we want—we want not for themselves but for the things they can *get* us (which things, in turn, we may either want for themselves or for the things *they* can get us.) So you see, "want" is a very vague word. (It's also a very common word. We say "I want" or "I don't want" dozens of times a day.)

OK, then. One way to categorize wants is to divide them up into conditional wants and ultimate wants. Conditional wants are the things I desire not for themselves but for other things they can get me. I want to wash your dishes for you. I also don't want to because I hate doing dishes. What I really want is to do something nice for you. So my desire to do your dishes is a conditional want. That is, it's something that I want not for itself but for something else it offers—a chance to do something for you.

An ultimate want, on the other hand, is something you want for itself. In other words, it's an end in itself (not just a means to an end). There are several implications to be drawn from all this. First of all, everything you do is something you want to do. "But I'm scrubbing the kitchen floor and I don't want to do that." Yes you do—otherwise, why would you be doing it? "I'm only doing it because I can't stand a dirty floor." Well, then you *want* to do cleaning for what that will give you. It's a conditional want. "OK, but I'd rather have someone else come in and clean my floor for me." Well, then, why don't you? "Because I don't have the money to hire someone." OK then, you would like someone else to do your cleaning, *but*—given the world the way it is, without the extra money, you also want to scrub your floor so that it will be clean. You wouldn't be doing it otherwise. Look at everything that you do in your life and you'll see that it's something you want to do. Look at everything you have and you'll see that it's something you want to have—otherwise you'd throw it away. If you own something you don't want at all, then ask yourself why it is that you're keeping it. Once you can answer that question you'll either throw it away or else you'll know why you want it. (In case it sounds shocking to you to hear that every thing you have or do is something you want, don't worry—many of those things that you want you also *don't* want!)

Of course, all of this is really no big deal. Some people go around these days saying "You want to do everything you do" as if that's something profound. It's about as profound as saying "Everything that exists is real" or "All numbers are mathematical." Big deal. So if someone says to you, "Everything you do, you want to do," tell her "So what." But if someone says to you, "There's nothing you do that you don't want to do," tell him he's wrong. Because there are many things you do that you don't want to do. Just because you also *want* to do them doesn't mean you can't *not* want to do them at the same time.

The strange thing about all this is that it isn't always possible to figure out what your ultimate wants are. In the example I gave earlier the conditional want was to work. But what is it you're working for? To get money? But the money isn't something you want for itself. Even the things your money buys, you may not want for themselves. If you try to figure out just exactly what it is you want for itself, you may not be able to put your finger on anything at all. Think about that for a moment. Do you actually know what things you really want—your ultimate wants, the things you want for themselves? When you buy a car, is the car the thing you want for itself, or is it the transportation it provides? But is it the transportation in itself that you really want, or is it the places and activities to which the transportation brings you? But is it the places and activities or is it something the places and activities get you, like fun or excitement? But is it fun or excitement that you want for itself, or something one of these can give you (like some kind of physiological experience)?

I don't know about you, but I'm not sure I really *know* what it is that I want for itself. There are some things, like love and happiness, that seem to come closer to being ends in themselves than, say, a carton of milk. But I'm not sure whether love or happiness is what I ultimately want or whether they are also means to some other unconscious ends. (And besides, who knows just what "love" or "happiness" really is, anyway?)

One more thing about conditional versus ultimate wants: If you want to be happier, try pushing your conditional wants more up the scale to ultimate wants. That is, the things you have been wanting only for what they can get you, start wanting more for themselves. Life will be less of a drag that way. See if you can enjoy your job for itself, not just for the money you earn. Want to wash your dishes just for the pleasure of watching them come clean. Let yourself enjoy driving to the store or riding the bus or waiting for a doctor appointment. Want to mail a letter just for the fun of it; enjoy vacuuming the carpet just for the thrill. If you choose to think it's impossible to change your conditional wants to things you want for themselves, then go ahead and don't do anything. If, however, you want more fun and fulfillment, then you'll have to want to change the way you want. Your decision either way is OK with me, if that matters to you!

There. I have bothered to discuss different kinds and degrees of wants so that you will understand that this simple word which we use so often has more than one level of meaning. Most people are not aware of this—simply because they don't take the time to think about it. Now that *you* are aware of the different degrees and kinds of wants, you will be more clear about why you do what you do. And that clarity will give you more freedom. (Or, to be more accurate, that clarity will help you see the freedom that you already have but which you haven't been acknowledging or using.)

And now that you are more clear about the complexities of your wants, you are ready to go on to learn methods for doing those things that you want to get done.

7

How to Get Things Done That You've Been Putting Off: A Two-Step Process

How many things have you been wanting to get done but just haven't gotten around to doing? A letter you've been planning to write, a trip you've wanted to take but haven't gotten yourself together for, a book you've wanted to read but just haven't found the time for—I'm sure you could make up your own list. In fact, I'm going to ask you to think of one thing right now that you've been wanting to do but have been putting off...

That's right. Think of one small thing—something you could get done right now—that you've been meaning to do but haven't done yet...

Have you thought of something? If not, please do. You will find this exercise valuable...

OK, now I'm going to ask you to do an experiment with me. I'm going to ask you to get up right now and *do* that thing that you've been putting off.

I mean it! You can learn something from this, so go ahead, close this book, and *do* whatever it is you haven't gotten around to doing before.

* * * * * * * * * * * * * * *

There. Did you do that thing that you've been meaning to do? If you did, then you have just learned how to get things done that you've been putting off!

But if you're like most people, you probably didn't want to bother getting up to do it and so here you are, still reading. But you can learn something from that too. If you plan on doing something but end up not doing it, you learn this: You apparently didn't want to do it very much. (At least not as much as you wanted to *not* do it. As I explained in the last chapter, it's possible to want something and not want it at the same time because one of the wants is greater than the other.)

How do you know that you've been putting this thing off because you didn't want to do it very much? It's simple. If you *did* want to do it, you would have done it. But you didn't do it. So you must not have wanted to do it.

Here you've been going through life telling yourself that you just haven't gotten so many of those things done that you wanted—when the truth is, you just haven't wanted to do them very much. Oh, you're clever about it. You almost make it seem as though something were blocking your way. "I have a problem," you say. "I just can't get things done." That's a fantastic excuse. You make it seem that there's something outside of you—a "problem." You're just not doing it. There isn't anybody holding you back but yourself. You're not doing it because you don't want to do it. That's it. That's the truth. Don't lie about it.

You know, I saw a poster once which went something like this: "A Round Tuit: Buy one here and you will get ever so much done." Oh yes, people have been saying for centuries that they could get things done if only they could get "a round tuit." They don't want to admit—even to themselves—that they're not doing things because they're not doing things. "They," by the way, is you and me. *We* pretend we have a "problem"; we need a "tuit"—round kind, preferably—and then we will succeed. Yes, don't blame *me*; it's not *my* fault—I just never got one of those hypothetical instruments, the tuit (circular variety, please).

To see how silly our excuses sound, I'd like you to look at a few examples of how we evade responsibility with them:

"Don't worry, I'll get the job done—as soon as I get a round tuit." (Yeah, but what if they run out of them by the time you get down to the hardware store—*then* what will you do?)

"I would just love to take that fantastic vacation trip around the world, but I just never seem to get a round tuit." (Oh, so you've got everything *else* planned and ready to go. Now all you need is one of those tuits so they'll let you out of the country, right?)

"Jean, I'm angry that you didn't do what you promised. Why didn't you get it done?" "Well, you see, I *intended* to, but I just never got a round tuit." (Oh, is *that* why. Well, that's not your fault then. How could I have ever thought of blaming you? Here I thought you failed to keep your promise. Now I see that you were just missing a vital ingredient, the tuit. Certainly not your fault—I'll get you one right away.)

Now do you see what your excuses are doing? They're making it seem that there's some mysterious force out there keeping you from doing what you want. "I don't know what's wrong with me—I just can't seem to get things done." It sounds almost mystical, doesn't it? "I have a problem with putting things off." (Oh, well then, maybe we'd better look into your childhood and explore your dreams so that we can find out the nature of it.)

You see, the word "problem" doesn't add anything here. And "didn't get around to it" doesn't add anything either. "I have a *problem* getting things done" merely means "I'm not getting things done." Period. "I didn't do it because I didn't get around to it" merely means "I didn't do it." Period again. All you're adding when you say you have a problem or that you didn't get around to it—is an illusion. Look at those sentences again: "I'm having a problem getting things done." It almost sounds as if the "problem" is *causing* you to not get things done. Or: "I didn't do it because I didn't get around to it.'' The word "because" makes it sound as though not-getting-around-to-it *caused* you to not do it. (Much the same as the "because" does in this sentence: "I didn't make it to the meeting on time because I had a flat tire"—in other words, the flat tire caused the delay.) But the truth is, nothing is *causing* you to not do it. You're just not doing it, and you're pretending that some problem or force "out there" is stopping you. There's nothing mystical or magical or mysterious about the fact that you're not getting things done. You're just not getting them done. That's all there is tuit!

I hope all you would-be dieters and exercisers get this, by the way. If you're not dieting or exercising, even though you say you want to, it's not because you have a "problem" with these. It's because you're not doing them. All you have to do to diet is not eat as much. Very simple. Why make it so mysterious? ("I'm *trying* to, but I just can't control myself.") You can do it. It may be difficult. It may hurt your tummy. But you can do it. Stop pretending that some weird force is coming in and taking over your body—when the truth is, you would rather be fat than have the inconvenience of dieting or exercising.

The reason you and other people plan on doing things and then don't do them is that you don't want to *admit* that you don't really want to do them. That way you can look good to other people (or to yourself). For example, someone suggests a book for you to read and you want to appear intelligent or cultured, so you say you'll read it "when you have time"—and then you don't. "Yes, I'll have to read that," you say. And then you conveniently don't get a round tuit. How clever. That way you don't have to say the truth: "Thanks for the suggestion, but I don't think I'll want to read it." (Oh my God, maybe they'll *hate* you for not wanting to read a book they liked.)

Suppose you believe that really "informed" and "enlightened" people read *Time* or *Newsweek*, or at least they read the newspaper everyday (or at least watch the news on

TV?)—and maybe you don't do any of these things. So, because you don't want to seem like a real dolt, you keep telling yourself that you'll just *have* to get in the habit of doing these things—"eventually." And you never do. But you're always *intending* to and *planning* to. Intending and planning aren't doing. They're just intending and planning. And when they're not followed by doing, then they're pretty worthless exercises indeed.

But they make you look good (or at least you think they do). So you go around not doing things that you supposedly want to do and you keep *saying* you want to do them and pretending that something is keeping you from doing them—so that you won't have to admit that you don't really want to do them (otherwise you'd be doing them) and look silly.

The pay-off is that you get to look good to other people and to yourself, and you never have to displease anyone (because you can always agree to do what anyone wants and then just not get around to it). The price you pay, however, is feeling guilty or incompetent for not accomplishing what you set out to do. For example, everybody knows you're supposed to give your family and friends gifts on their birthdays and at Christmas time, right? Only, some of us forget, year after year, and feel guilty year after year. I used to have that "problem." Then I decided not to bother anymore. I made an agreement with my friends that I just wasn't going to give gifts at the expected times anymore. Not even cards. And, wonder of wonders, the world didn't end as a result. So now, except for my parents, I don't buy cards or gifts anymore. I'm doing what I always did, only now I'm admitting the truth—that I used to "forget" to send gifts because I never really *wanted* to send them (at least not very much). And I don't feel guilty anymore.

I'm not suggesting that *you* give up sending gifts, by the way. Send them or don't send them. Do whatever you want to do. Just be honest about what you do or don't want to do. For your own sake, *and* that of your friends and family.

OK, now you're ready to learn the two-step process for getting things done, although I've been talking about it all along *and you've known it all your life*. The two-step process for getting things done is this: 1) Decide, and 2) do.

Simple, isn't it? Decide and do. What could be easier? So far, you've probably been able to manage step 1 (you've been deciding to do things all your life). It's step 2 that you're not accomplishing. But there's nothing else I can tell you about doing. You're either doing or you're not doing. I can't give you a pill that will *make* you do things that you're not already doing. How do you get yourself to do things? You just do them, that's all.

Now, suppose you decide to, say, mow your lawn. And then you don't do it. Well, then, you've learned something: you obviously didn't want to mow your lawn very much (at least not as much as you wanted to *not* mow your lawn). But hold it. You're not through yet. After you acknowledge the fact that you didn't mow your lawn because you didn't want to, you have a new choice open to you (you *always* have choices open to you): Do you *now* want to mow your lawn? I mean, it's obvious you didn't want to *then*. But how about *now*? If your answer is yes, then decide to do it and then do it.

It should be clear that a person's wants can change from moment to moment. Right now I want an ice-cream cone. Now I remember I'm on a diet and so I decide I'd rather not. But who knows what I'll want in the next "moment of now"? Or in the moment after that? So even though it's true that if you didn't get things done it's because you didn't want to—still you can always choose to change your mind *now* and finally really get them done.

Here's an example. I used to go around forgetting to do things. I mean, someone would say, "Hey, why don't you read this book?" or "Can you talk to So-and-so about this?"—and I would say yes but then forget to do it. So I thought about it and came up with an idea: I could write down these things on slips of paper that I would keep in my appointment book, and I could refer to them from time to time. Gee, that sounded like a great idea. All I needed was to cut up some slips of paper and put them in my appointment book.

And I didn't do it. So then I said to myself, "I'll have to put some slips of paper in my book very soon."

And I didn't do it. So then I said to myself, "Gee, I wonder why I haven't done this yet. I'd really better get some of those slips of paper for my appointment book."

And I didn't do it. So then I told myself a fantastic lie: "Gee, I certainly have a *problem* with this."

But this time I caught myself in my game and I realized that I didn't really want to *bother* getting slips of paper and putting them in my little book. I realized that I apparently didn't *care* that much about remembering to do things.

And you know what? The sky didn't fall in, the world didn't collapse, and I didn't die. I realized that it's *OK* to not always remember everything.

Now, my story could have ended here. But it didn't. Once I accepted the fact that I didn't really want to get those slips of paper—*then* I was free to realize that *now* I did want to start using those slips of paper. Interesting, eh? If I hadn't realized that I didn't want to do it, I probably would have gone on not doing it and wondering what my problem was. But when I realized that I didn't want to do it, and *accepted* that, then I was free to re-examine my wants and change them. Anyway, I've been carrying around slips of paper in my appointment book ever since, and remembering to do a lot more than I ever did before. (I may change my mind in the future and stop carrying paper with me, but that will be OK if it happens. Right *now* I want to carry it around, and my want now is what's important now.)

You know what's really funny about my slips of paper? Everytime I tell people about it, they say, "Oh, you're so well organized. I wish I could be that way." Isn't that crazy? They think I have a trait or quality called "organizational ability" which they don't have. They look at my behavior and then say that I must have some trait or quality which causes the behavior or makes it possible. They're doing the same thing with efficient behavior that they do with inefficient behavior. They invent something—a quality or a trait—to use as an explanation for the deed. But that's just mystical nonsense. Just as there's no "problem" keeping you from doing what you want or any "round tuit" that you have to get before you can do anything—there's also no quality called "organizational ability" which I have but they don't have. I don't have *any*thing in this area that they don't have. I'm just *doing* things differently than they are. They could do the same things if they wanted to. All they need to do is make an act of the will. *Any*body can do that.

But people don't want to admit that. They'd rather pretend they're lacking some elusive quality than admit that they're not doing it because they don't want to.

"She does so many kind things for people. I sure wish I could." Crazy. *Any*body could. *You* could. You just don't want to admit that it's more bother than you care to take on, so you pretend that she has some "thing" called kindness, which causes the kind deeds. (And since you don't have that thing in you, of course you can't.) Cop-out. She doesn't have some thing called kindness. Kindness is a name we use to describe a person *after* we see the nice things she does. It's not a cause of the behavior; it's a response to the behavior—a label. It doesn't exist in itself.

The same is true of will power. "He always does what he sets out to do. He's got more will power than I do." Nonsense. He doesn't have anything you don't have. He's *doing* things differently from you. You just don't want to believe that.

Responsibility. It merely means acting in a mature way. Anyone can do it, once she or he knows what's the responsible thing to do. All you need to do is choose to do it. Being organized, being kind, being responsible, and having determination or will power—they are all matters of choice. If you're missing some of these, it's not because you're lacking something. It's because you're choosing to *act otherwise*.

That's all.

Here are a few more examples of how I have used the decide-and-do process for getting things done. Not long ago a friend of mine gave me some books to read that I was mildly interested in. I took them home and they promptly began gathering dust on my bookshelf. "Gee, I really should read those," I said to myself.

And I didn't. "Uh-oh, I'd better get to those sometime or he's going to wonder what happened," I thought.

And I didn't read them. Months passed. Everytime I looked at those books I felt guilty. (Actually, with all the time I wasted thinking about how I really *should* read them and all the moments I used up "planning" to read them "eventually"—I probably could have gotten some of them read!)

Finally I realized that the reason I wasn't reading them now and probably never would—was that I didn't really *want* to. So I brought them back to my friend and said, "Here are your books. I really don't think I'll get around to reading them, so I thought I'd better return them." (Of course, if I had been more honest, I would have admitted that I just didn't want to read them instead of using the "round tuit" excuse.) Fortunately, my friend understood.

Another time an acquaintance gave me three books to read that he was sure I would find fascinating. Well, the same thing happened. I kept putting it off and feeling worse and worse about my "problem." In this case, however, I didn't want to admit to the person who loaned me the books that I didn't read them. I also didn't want to lie and say I did if I didn't. So I took an hour to skim through parts that looked vaguely interesting and then left a note with the books for him that said: "Thanks for the opportunity to look these over. I read parts of them and found them interesting." (That wasn't a lie. I did find them interesting—mostly because I decided to make myself interested.)

Now some people would criticize me for wasting an hour of my time reading something I wasn't very interested in—instead of simply admitting to the person who loaned me the books that I didn't read them because I didn't want to. Some would also criticize me for leaving a note instead of confronting the man personally. I obviously took the "chicken" way out. And you know what? I feel OK about that! So what if I wasn't what others would call "assertive"? I don't *have* to do the more bold or courageous thing just because some outside authority says I should. In the end, it is more assertive to do what *you* want, whether that's the "chicken" way or not, rather than be bound by other people's rules for how you can be more "healthy" or "adjusted."

So you see, the important thing in this example is not *what* I did or whether you would have done the same thing. The important thing is that I did what I wanted to do. And what's important for *you* is that you do what *you* want. Decide and do. And then if you end up not doing it, you know that you didn't really want to. And then you can decide *again* whether you *now* want to do it or not. Life is a series of decide-and-do, decide-and-do, over and over forever.

The neat thing about the D&D method is that it's something you can do right now to improve your life. I mean, you can forget what I said in Part One about changing your attitudes and you can skip Part Three, where I talk about feelings. You can even believe that *things* have the power to make you happy or sad (though of course they don't). All you need to do is start deciding to do the things you think will "make" you happy and then start doing them. That's why this chapter is probably the easiest to apply in the whole book. You don't need any special qualities or therapeutic techniques or extra time to apply D&D. Just D&D!

In my courses on becoming an effective person, I ask the students to make a list of things they want to accomplish during the week and then I have them report on their success at the following class. It is almost always uplifting to watch people improve their lives by simply deciding to do so. One woman reported that she got a number of household chores and other tasks accomplished during the week, which she felt good about. "I just felt so motivated, I couldn't help but get things done." I pointed out to her, however, that the D&D method works *regardless* of your mood or motivation. You don't have to feel anything in order to get things accomplished. In fact, the greater challenge is to get things done when you feel depressed or tired or "under the weather." It may be harder, but you *can* do that if you choose to. (As a matter of fact, I usually keep a list of routine or perfunctory tasks that I'd like to get accomplished but which don't need special concentration or creativity, like typing, cleaning, etc. Then when I feel low I start doing some of these things, so that the time of feeling low is not used just for feeling low. Sometimes the good feeling of accomplishment I get even helps me overcome my bad feelings!) To do needs nothing other than the decision to do. Not motivation. Not good feelings. Not "good vibes." All you need in order to do is to decide to do and then to do.

So how about it? Are you ready to make your life more effective by just deciding to act more effectively? If you are, here are some hints.

First, make a list of things you would like to accomplish which would improve your life. Why a list? Because it's too easy otherwise to forget about the whole thing. Drawing up a list forces you to think of specific things that will enhance living.

After you've made your list, select just a few items that you can accomplish within the next week. It's important that you pick only a few, for openers, because if you choose too many for your first try, you may not get them all done, and then as a result you'll feel disappointed and frustrated—and perhaps give up on the whole idea. (You can always do more than you agree to, if you want. But keep your agreement manageable.) For the same reasons, your first items should be simple ones, easy to accomplish—like cleaning your bathroom, writing a few letters, buying a few things you want, etc. It's also important that you establish a time-line for your tasks—that is, fix a certain date or time by which you expect to accomplish the things on your list. That way you can check on yourself to see if you got what you wanted accomplished.

Another consideration for a beginning list is that your items should be things that don't need special circumstances. For example, deciding that "the next time Mary calls to invite me over for bridge, I'm not going to let her manipulate me into going"—is not a good idea for the beginning. It may take weeks before Mary calls you up, and by that time you may have forgotten about your agreement with yourself. A better first item would be to call Mary up today (or tomorrow) and tell her you won't make it to the next bridge party. Decide on things that don't have to wait for the "right time"—fill your list with do-able-at-any-time items.

Finally, your list should be made up of very specific things. If they are general, you'll never be sure whether you accomplished them or not. And you won't get the satisfaction of knowing you did something to handle your world more effectively. For example, deciding that you will be nicer to people from now on—is practically meaningless. When you come to the end of the day, how will you really know whether you were nice, in general, or not? A more specific item would be deciding to say at least three kind things each day to people. At the end of the day you'll know whether you accomplished that or not.

"From now on I'm going to be more assertive" is too vague. "I'm going to write/call Scotty and tell her my decision on this" is simple, clear, and to the point.

"I'm going to lose weight and start exercising" is too general. "I'm going to eat 2,000 calories or less, do 25 sit-ups, and jog 5 blocks every day" is workable because it's measurable.

"I'm going to start liking myself from now on" is a ridiculous statement. For one thing, no one either completely likes or completely dislikes herself. Self-esteem is never a matter of all-or-nothing. All you can do is learn to like yourself *more* than you do at present. But even that is too vague to be a good item. Try this instead: "I'm going to remind myself three times a day of at least 5 things I like about myself."

Those are my suggestions for doing more effectively. Make a list of items you would like to accomplish which are 1) few, 2) easy, 3) do-able-at-any-time, 4) specific (measurable), and which 5) can be accomplished within a certain time-line.

Isn't it great to know that you can get things done by simply choosing to do them? Even if, as a result of reading this chapter, you don't decide to do one thing to improve your life—isn't it fantastic to know that *you could if you wanted to*? And that the fact that you're not means you're *already* doing exactly what you want?

You do have the power to do what you choose. Use it!

8

I'll Try, I Hope

In this chapter I want to warn you about two barriers that you are probably erecting to fool yourself into not doing things. The two barriers are the expressions *I'll try* and *I hope*.

"Will you get hold of Ellen for me?" "I'll try."

"Will you be at the meeting tonight?" "I'll try."

"My life isn't working, but I'm *trying* to change."

You know what the problem is with the word "try"? It doesn't say anything. If you ask people to come to a meeting and they say, "I'll try," do you know whether they're coming to the meeting or not? No. All you know is that they're making an effort, whatever that means. If you ask Ellen to contact Bob and she says, "I'll try," do you know whether she'll get hold of Bob or not? No. She may call him once and if there's no answer she won't call again. Or she may call twice. Or she may be content with writing a letter or leaving a message. She may even never get around to calling him once. After all, she only said she'd try—which is just about the same as saying nothing.

"But I'm trying to change." Yes, but what specifically are you doing to change? Are you doing more of this, controlling more of that? Or are you just, in general, "trying"? You know, you can grunt and groan and sigh and say, "oh-o-oh, I'm making such an effort, I'm trying so hard"—but if you're not doing anything then you're not doing anything. Let me run that one by you again in case you missed it: If you're not really doing anything then you're not really doing

anything—no matter how much you groan or grit your teeth.
Of course, it's very convenient to try at everything. No one
can blame you for not getting anything done. "Well, I tried. I
didn't do anything, but I *tried* at not doing anything."

"Can you make it tomorrow to help us?" "Well, I'll
try"—which often means, "Gee, I really don't want to, but
I'd better not admit it. And besides, there's an outside
chance everything else will be so boring that I just might
make it."

Instead of saying, "I'll try to make the meeting," why not
say, "I *will* be there" and then be there, or "I won't be
there," or "I don't know if I will or not."

Instead of saying, "I'll try to contact Bob," why not say,
"Well, I'll call him and if he's not there I'll call again at least
once." Or "I'll call him twice and if he doesn't answer I'll
write him a note." That says something concrete. Instead of
saying, "Hey, it's New Year's, and I'm going to try to be
better," why not say, "This year I will say three kind things a
week to my in-laws, take my spouse out to dinner twice a
month, and hold back on the bitter, sarcastic comments I
normally make to the people I work with. I'm not going to try
to do these things. I'm going to do them."

Oh, most of us are great at promising to try. That's the
most convenient kind of promise to make because it isn't a
promise to do anything. It's a way of pretending to commit
yourself to something. Instead of saying honestly, "I won't
do this," or "I don't want to do this," or "I don't know if I
will do this or not," we say, "I'll try"—as if *we* are perfectly
willing to do it but there are all these outside forces holding
us back.

Now I'm not saying we should drop the word "try" from
our vocabulary. There is a sense of the word that we haven't
been discussing here. Sometimes "to try" means to
experiment, as when we say we'll try a new food. But in the
examples I've been exploring, at its best this expression is
just short-hand for saying, "I don't know if I will do this or
not but if nothing else more desirable comes up for me, I

will.'' At its worst, the expression deludes ourselves and others into thinking we've said something or promised something when we haven't. Don't ever believe you're saying anything that can be pinned down when you say you'll try to do something. ''I'm going to try to swim'' doesn't say anything concrete. (It could mean you're going to shiver at the edge of the pool ''trying'' to get psyched up.) Now, ''I'm going to splash my hands around in the water like my swim instructor showed me'' does say something. ''I'm going to try to learn French'' doesn't say anything. ''I'm going to study this French book'' does. When you use a vague word like ''try'' you open yourself up to letting fate or whim take over your life. Worse, you let chance take over without realizing it.

Next expression: *I hope*. ''I hope it doesn't rain.'' ''I hope I'll be alive tomorrow.'' ''I hope I make it on time.'' As far as I can see, there are two kinds of hope: Hoping and having hope. ''I hope that things will turn out all right'' is different from ''I have hope that things will turn out all right.'' ''I have hope'' means ''I am confident, I am not in despair.'' It's an attitude, a way of looking. And it is, I believe, basically healthy. It helps us when we face tragedy. It gives direction to our life—it sets a focus for our goals. We have hope for a better life, a better world—in other words, we have an attitude about life. To have hope is productive. It doesn't waste your time because it's not something you keep saying to yourself, like ''I hope, I hope, I hope.''

To just hope, on the other hand, is usually unproductive. ''I hope this happens'' is not an attitude; it's a time-consuming mental process. ''I hope she liked what I bought her. I hope I don't have an accident. I hope I'll have fun tonight.'' Saying ''I hope'' is unproductive for two reasons. First, when you hope for good things and they don't happen, you're disappointed. A healthy optimist, by the way, is *not* a person who hopes for the best—but a person who doesn't hope, and then is pleasantly surprised when things turn out nicely.

The second reason that hoping is unproductive (hoping—not having hope) is that it simply doesn't accomplish anything. No matter how much you hope for something, reality will go its own merry way. When you were a child, you probably thought, "Maybe if I hope and hope, it will come true." You should know better now, but this childhood belief in magic may still be influencing the way you act, so let me remind you as forcefully as I can: Reality will not be changed by your hoping. Reality will do what it will do regardless of how much you hope otherwise. Hoping has no effect on what happens in the outside world. It's like trying. You can try and try. And you can hope and hope. But trying to do something isn't doing that thing—it's just trying. And hoping isn't doing anything either—it's just hoping. If you want to do something, do something. Hoping won't accomplish that something for you. About the only thing it does is take up your time. I hope, I hope, I hope. It's about as useful as worrying. As a matter of fact, it's the reverse of worrying. Worrying is thinking that things might turn out badly. Hoping is thinking that things might turn out well. But thinking either way has no effect on how things will actually turn out. As a matter of fact, worrying and hoping are often interchangeable. "I hope the sun shines tomorrow" often means "(But) I'm worried that it might rain." "I hope my boss gives me a raise" often means "(But) I'm worried that she won't."

I'm not suggesting that you drop the word "hope" from your vocabulary. As I've said, to *have* hope is healthy. And we oftentimes say "I hope" as an expression of concern rather than a wasteful mental process—as, for example, when we say to a friend, "I hope things turn out all right for you." That expression doesn't really mean that you're thinking and thinking that things might turn out OK—it just means "I care about you," and it's perfectly appropriate. It's the hope-hope-hope kind of hope that I'm talking about here, which sets you up for disappointments when it isn't fulfilled. Even when it doesn't do that, it still doesn't get anything accomplished. Why waste your time hoping?

If you remember what I said earlier about *need, have to,
don't have the time, can't* and *but*, and now about *I'll try* and
I hope, you'll be able to change the following statement to get
rid of its implicit barriers to freedom:

"I can't get involved because I don't have the time, I have
to do other things. I hope to get involved sometime and I'll
try, but I need time for other things right now."

Change that to: "I don't want to get involved, because I
don't want to take time away from other things that are more
important to me. I want to do those other things. It's possible
that I will want to get involved at a later date (I'm not hoping
anything), so I'll consider that possibility in a year or two
(rather than promise to 'try'). I want time for other things
more, right now."

That's more honest. And it allows you to be more free. Or
rather, by considering your wants more honestly, *you* allow
yourself to be more free. After all, you are the one who is
going to make the difference in your life. Reality will go its
merry way, so if you want more happiness and freedom,
you'd better make some changes in how you look at reality.
Reality will not make things different just for you. You must
make the difference.

And you can! Trust yourself!

9

Stop Being Manipulated

OK, you're going to do some important things *for yourself.*
You've decided to change your life. How will you deal with
other people's attempts to *stop* you? Although other people
usually do not have the power to stop you, you often believe
they do and then let yourself be "conned" into doing what
you don't want. (However, even when you are "conned," you
are still doing what you *want*—because you *want* to do what
you *don't want* more than you want to go against someone
else's wishes and risk an "incident." Obviously, it's quite
possible to do something that you want *and* don't want at the
same time because of different levels of wants.)

What I want to do in this chapter is help you to understand
what is happening when someone manipulates you; show you
that *you have the power* to not let yourself be manipulated;
and give you some practical suggestions on what to say and
do when manipulative situations occur. However, I also want
to say at the outset that you also have the right to *let* people
make your decisions for you if you think you will be happier
that way. (After all, some people will be nicer to you if you let
them have their way most of the time, and if you want that,
then choose it. I just want you to know that that *is* a
choice—you don't *have* to be manipulated into fulfilling other
people's wishes. If you end up giving up what you want at
someone else's insistence, know that at a higher level of want
you *wanted* to give it up—you must have wanted it because
you did it after all, didn't you?)

Letting other people manipulate you (or "pull your

strings") must be a common malady these days because there are certain standard expressions we use that reveal it. For example, "She talked me into it." Now look at that sentence for a moment. What does it mean to get "talked into" something? Either the person reasoned with you so that it made sense to you and *you* decided to do it (in which case you weren't really *talked* into it—you just made a choice on the basis of the evidence offered to you). *Or,* you did something you didn't want to do because you didn't want to bother resisting the person's arguments or manipulations (in which case it wasn't her *talking* that made you do it—it was your unwillingness to assert your own wants that allowed *you* to do it. Obviously, not everyone *else* does things that other people tell them to, so when *you* do, it must be because you choose it.) In other words, no one else has the power to talk you into anything—you just think they do; it's easier to accept that than to admit the truth: that you do some pretty dumb things because you want to (or at least you want to more than you want to insist on your own rights).

Look at some other expressions which we use to kid ourselves that we had no choice: "I got roped into it." (Oh, did someone force you with a lassoo?) "I got hooked into it." (Ouch, that must have hurt.) "They dragged me into it." (Really? How long did it take them to subdue you?)

All of these are examples of how we pretend someone else made us do something...when the truth of the matter is that *we went along.* We *agreed* to be roped, hooked, dragged, conned. There was no roping or dragging at all, actually—we were just agreeing to do what someone else said we should do.

It's amazing. Why do we give people power over us? Sometimes we give in to other people's ideas and wishes because we think they will love us if we do. "If I just go their way, maybe they'll think I'm OK." If we give in to other people's decisions about what to do, then we don't have to take the blame if things go wrong. "But it was her idea—she told me to." If we act helpless, we think people will take care of us. "I give up. I can't do anything. Now someone else will have to do it for me." If we refuse to make a decision, we never have to feel we made the wrong one. Oh yes, there are plenty of reasons for doing what others want instead of choosing for ourselves. But often there is something going on at the other end—that is, often the other person is saying or doing things that "make" us feel we have to go along. In a word, manipulation. If you understand what is going on, it will be easier to guard against it.

So let's look at what is going on. As far as I can see, in most situations where another person gets us to do something we don't want to do, the person 1) does something that we feel decides for us; 2) "convinces" us that our way "doesn't make sense" or "isn't reasonable"; or 3) "convinces" us that we would be bad (selfish, heartless, crazy) if we did things our way.

Some examples of no. 1: You're at a party or a bar and someone says, "Have another drink." You say, "No thanks," but the other says, "Aw, come on," and pours you one anyway. You know this kind of person—genial Joe. He's just being *nice*, right? At least that's what he would tell you. Only he has completely disregarded your wishes, which is a strange way of being nice. So now there's another drink there and perhaps you think you can't do anything about it. You don't want to be *rude*, after all. (But did you ever consider how rude it was of *him* to ignore your want?) So you just "have to" drink it.

Wrong. You don't have to do anything. You can leave the drink there. You can even be "nice" about it if you want—smile and say thanks and don't make a big deal about it, but *don't drink it*. Joe didn't force you to do anything by giving you an extra drink—he didn't pour it down your throat, did he? Be honest with yourself: *you have a choice*.

Another example: I was at a party one evening and someone offered me a piece of cake. I wasn't hungry and said, "No thanks." The man "insisted" that I have it, however, and put a plate of cake in my hands. Now, I could have not put out my hands to take it, and just let him hold it in front of me as I looked at him strangely—but I thought that might be being too hard on him. So I just accepted it—and then set it down on a nearby table. You see, it's possible to not let yourself be manipulated and still not appear rude! He got my point, and he even offered an apology later. All you people who want to lose weight, learn from this. You don't have to eat just because everyone else is doing it and "insisting." You can refuse, *with grace*. No belligerence necessary—just don't, and make no big deal about it.

Here are two more examples of manipulation, type no. 1, and how to deal with it: You're out at a restaurant with someone who orders something for you that you don't want. "Oh, you'll love it," she says. "No thanks," you answer. But she orders it for you anyway. Are you then forced into having it? No, you can either calmly tell the waitress or waiter that you don't want it, or else just not eat or drink it when it comes. If the other person later asks why you haven't touched it, you can even be very nice about it and say, "Oh, would you have it? I really don't want any." I mean, if you want, you can act as if it wasn't anyone's fault that the unwanted food just "appeared" on the table. That's how nice you can be. (Careful here, though; don't be *patronizing*!) So if you're worried that exercising your freedom of choice will seem rude to someone who tries to get you to do what you don't want—then this and the other examples should show you that it is usually possible to assert your rights in a way that doesn't put the other person down. (Of course, if you *want* to make a big point of your rights and embarrass the other person, then that is your choice too. Somehow I have the feeling you won't.)

Now here's a toughie: Suppose you and a friend are trying to agree on a movie (or restaurant or other entertainment place) and your friend, who happens to be driving the car, brings you both to the place where *he* wants to go. Uh-oh. You're *there*. It seems as if you have no alternative but to accept the entertainment *he* chose.

Not so. If it's important enough to you, you can say (nicely, if you want), "I can see that you really want to go to this movie/restaurant. But I would rather not, so why don't you go ahead and I'll meet you later"—that is, if you *want* to meet him later after this number he's tried to pull on you. Or, "I can see you've made up your mind on this place, but I've got another in mind. Go ahead—don't worry about me. I can take a bus/cab/walk to where I'm going." If you say this in a calm, nonjudgmental voice, it's amazing to see the reaction from the other person.

You may also want to develop your own styles of "negotiation" for dealing with such situations, so that you may achieve some compromise with the other person: "OK, we'll go here tonight, but next week the choice is mine." In either case, it's amazing to see how good you can feel (powerful, too) when you assert yourself without putting someone else down.

In the above examples I've discussed a way to handle situations in which someone does something that seems to force a decision on you (pours a drink, orders for you). Now let's look at examples of a more common form of manipulation—the cases in which the other person tries to *talk* you out of what you want to do. Let's face it. People who manipulate others are not usually as bold as in the above situations; your more common problem will be with people who try to stop you by telling you that what you want isn't reasonable (type no. 2) or that you are somehow bad for wanting it (type no. 3).

"Why do you want to do that? I thought you had better judgment than to do something so irrational." When someone says that to you, what is your automatic reaction? If you're like most people, you start defending your rationality with lines like "I am *not* being irrational" or "What's so wrong with my judgment?" Then the other person proceeds to show you step by step how your decision isn't reasonable and *you* react by explaining how it is. Only problem is this: By your defending yourself you are in effect accepting their position that you can't do something *unless* it is "rational." As if only *rational* counts.

Actually, you can do whatever you want, no matter how unreasonable it seems to anyone else. It's your right. Not only that, but once you allow the debate over reasonableness to continue, you make it seem that whoever wins the debate gets to decide what you will do. Isn't that crazy? The issue is really what you want to do. But you let the issue become: who is the best debater? So in effect the person who has the best debating skills gets to decide what *you* will do—when the person who *should* decide what you will do...is you. Arguing skills have nothing to do with what you want to do.

The point I'm making here sounds so obvious that I would feel silly talking about it—if it weren't for the fact that people *do* let their decisions be made for them on the basis of debating ability! Look at the following manipulative conversation:

> You: "Well, I'm going shopping for awhile. See you later."
>
> Other: "Why are you going shopping?" (You never realized you were supposed to have a reason, but now that you're asked for one you feel obligated to give one. Instead of saying, "Oh, I just want to," you say:)
>
> Y: "Uh, well, there are some things I need to buy."
>
> O: "Oh, what do you need?" (Uh-oh. Think of something fast.)
>
> Y: "Just a few things—some soap, maybe a carton of milk."
>
> O: "Why don't you get the milk tomorrow? I noticed that you have enough to last till then in your refrigerator. And I've got plenty of soap you can use."
>
> Y: "Oh no, I couldn't think of using your soap." (You're hoping you can still go shopping.)
>
> O: "Nonsense. What are friends for? Now you just sit yourself down and I'll show you pictures of my trip. (Pause...as you still look anxious to leave.) There's

nothing else you *have* to get, is there? I mean, I don't want to *keep* you if you've got more *important* things to do." (A great hooker. Now you feel guilty for not *begging* to see the other's photographs.)
Y: "Oh no, you're right. Let's see what you have there."

Ho-hum. But whoever told you you had to have a reason to go shopping (or do anything else)—other than that you just want to?

Take a look at another manipulative conversation. This one is an example of type 3, in which the other person "convinces" you that you would be bad to do what you want.

Other: (Calls on the phone) "Come on out for awhile and have a few drinks with us."
You: "Uh, I don't think so. Maybe another time?"
O: "Hey-y-y-y, what's wrong?"
Y: "Nothing's wrong, I've just got other things to do." (Uh-oh, you'd better think of something fast, because you know what the next question is.)
O: "What could be so important to do on a Friday night?"
Y: "Well, I've got some cleaning to do and some reading."
O: "Hey, your friends are more important than that, aren't they?" (The old guilt trip.)
Y: "Well, sure, but—" (You've fallen for it, of course.)
O: "Come on out, then. Are we important to you or not?"
Y: "But I really had these other plans and—"
O: "Hey, I don't believe what I'm hearing. I can't believe you wouldn't think of your friends—I've never known you to be selfish before." (Ouch, you really got hit where it hurts, didn't you? You don't want anyone to think you're bad, cruel, heartless, *selfish!*)
Y: "Well, if it means that much, I guess I could go out for a little while."

O: "That's the spirit. Pick you up in a half hour." (And, of course, you won't be able to stay just a *little* while unless you arrange your own transportation home. Considering how you've fared so far, I doubt that you'll be assertive enough to leave the party early. Your friends will "insist" on driving you home—later. See what *you got yourself* into?)

Now, how about some remedies? Here are four different techniques you can use that will "take you off the hook" so-to-speak. The first is: Asking Objective Questions.

If people use criticism on you (telling you you're not "reasonable" or "nice," for example), then ask them to explain specifically what they mean—but ask in a curious way, not with sarcasm or a put-down (because that would be getting right into their game and fighting their criticism with criticism). Here's an example: Someone says, "Gee, it's selfish of you not to want to help your friends today." You answer, "Do you think so? In what way do you think it's selfish?" "Well, it's ungrateful not to want to help them out." "I'm not completely following you. How is it ungrateful?" "After all they've done for you, you owe them that much." "I don't understand. How do I owe them that?" And so on. By asking for objective reasons you can often stop manipulative criticism by exposing other people's biases or moral standards—*their* standards may not be your standards at all. You see, in order for people's criticism to hook you, it has to get you to fight back (by denying it or by using it back on the other person). But by asking objective questions about the criticism (how? in what way? why? could you be more specific?), you throw the ball back into the other's hands. The other criticizes in the hope of making you explain yourself; your objective questions throw the ball back so that the other person must explain his or her criticism.

There's something very important to get here. When people want to manipulate you, they normally ask you a lot of questions (Why do you want to do that? Have you ever tried it my way before? How do you know you wouldn't like it my way? Why are you being so selfish?). As soon as you start answering them you open yourself up to answering forever. That's because "how" and "why" questions have no ultimate answers. That is, for every answer you give to the question "why" or "how" — why or how can always be asked again. Every five-year-old knows this.

"Mommy, why can't I go on the rollercoaster?" "Because your father said no."

"But why did he say no?" "Because it's not safe for you."

"Why isn't it safe?" "Because it goes too fast."

"Why wouldn't that be safe?" "Because you might get hurt."

"How would I get hurt?" "You might fall out."

"How could that happen?" "Well, the seat belt might not hold you."

"But, Mommy, why wouldn't it?" "Oh God, I don't know. Your father said no and that's it."

It took a while for Mommy to catch on, didn't it. We could do the same thing with "how?" ("How do you walk?" I lift up my legs. "How do you do that?" Well, my brain sends a message through my nervous system. "How?" Uh, through electric current, sort of. "How does electric current work?" Got it?) But the neat thing about the technique of Asking Objective Questions is that *you* ask the *other* person the questions. You can't lose with that because the other won't be able to explain all of his or her arguments or criticisms. You just keep asking how or why or some other question. The other can never answer them all and will be kept on the defensive — instead of you.

Take another look at the conversation about shopping on page 78. Now see how it could have gone if you used the technique of Asking Objective Questions:

>   You: "Well, I'm going shopping for awhile. See you later."

>   Other: "Why are you going shopping?"

Y: "I just want to. Why do you ask?"

O: "Well, I just thought you must have something you need to buy."

Y: "Oh. Why would you think that?"

O: "Well, it just wouldn't make sense to go otherwise."

Y: "Really? Hm, why is that?"

O: "Well, people don't usually go shopping if they don't have anything to buy."

Y: "No? Why don't they?"

O: "Because there would be no reason to."

Y: "I don't understand. Why would they need a reason?"

O: "Well, people just don't *do* things without a reason."

Y: "I'm sorry. I'm afraid I'm not following you. Why wouldn't they?"

O: "You've got to be the dumbest person I've ever talked to." (Careful now—don't get sarcastic. Just calmly say, as if you were simply the most curious per- the world:)

Y: "Gee, I don't think I followed that. Could you be more specific?"

O: "Well, you're saying dumb things."

Y: "I don't think I follow you. What dumb things?"

O: "Everything you're saying is dumb."

Y: "I'm afraid I don't understand. Could you explain what you mean?"

Well, the conversation could go on—if you wanted to bother. If you'd like a more short-hand method, however, try a second technique: Accepting Criticism. When people try to manipulate you into doing their thing by criticizing you, don't fight it. Just admit whatever truth there is in their accusation and then state what you want to do. Someone says, "Boy, I can't believe how inconsiderate you are for not helping us out." You answer, "I can understand how it might seem inconsiderate, and actually I am sometimes inconsiderate of people, but this is what I want to do." "But it's so selfish." "Well, it may be, but that's what I want to do." "But it's such a dumb thing to do." "You may be right—I do a lot of dumb things—but I'll just have to find that out because that's what I want to do."

Do you see what happens when you accept criticism? The other person is using it to get you to deny it so that he or she can engage you in a debate (with the "winner" deciding what you do). Instead, you end the game by accepting the criticism. Simple. It doesn't have a chance to work against you. So the other person must try a new stone to throw. Which, again, you accept. And so on. Until eventually the other person gets tired of starting game after game, because you never play them—and the games don't work with only one player.

Let's say someone is trying to get some gossip out of you, or to find out something about you that you don't want to reveal. With your acceptance of their criticisms, the conversation might go like this:

Other: "Hey, what's the scoop? Let your old friend in on it, huh?"

You: "I don't really want to talk about it."

O: "Oh, come on, don't tell me you're *afraid* to talk about it."

Y: "That could be."

O: "Hey, you'll feel better if you unload. It's dumb to hold it in."

Y: "Well, that wouldn't be the first time I've done something dumb. I still don't want to talk about it, though."

O: "Don't you think it's rather selfish to keep things from your friends?"

Y: "I can see how it might seem that way, and sometimes I am selfish, but I still don't want to talk about it."

O: "Well, this just doesn't make sense."

Y: "Maybe it doesn't. I guess maybe it really doesn't

make sense to anyone else.''

O: "I think there's something wrong with you—you're neurotic.''

Y: "Well, I won't argue with you there. I certainly am.''

Look at what the other person called you—afraid, dumb, selfish, irrational, and neurotic. You could have fought back at any time and had a debate on your hands, winner take all. But you didn't. And you did what you wanted.

A third technique to use when someone tries to get you to do something you don't want is: Repeating Yourself. Just calmly say, over and over if necessary, what you want to do. Eventually the other person will get bored with the conversation and will give up trying to change your mind. Actually, this one is the quickest technique we've looked at so far, but it also can seem more rude than the first two, so use it with discretion. Here's an example: "Mary, I'd like you to buy a ticket to this charity.'' "Thanks for the offer, John, but I don't want to.'' "But it's for a really good cause.'' "Thanks but I don't want a ticket.'' "Well, I think you really should, Mary.'' "I can see that, but I don't want a ticket.'' "*Why* won't you buy one?'' "I simply don't want one.'' "That sounds pretty selfish to me, Mary.'' "I just don't want a ticket, John.''

Let's take the manipulative conversation on page 79 about going out for a few drinks and use the repeater technique:

Other: "Come on out for awhile and have a few drinks with us.''

You: "Thanks anyway, but I don't want to tonight.''

O: "Hey-y-y-y, what's wrong?''

Y: "I just don't want to.''

O: "What else could you want to do on a Friday night?''

Y: "I don't want to.''

O: "Why not?''

Y: "I really just don't want to.''

O: "Hey, aren't your friends important to you?''

Y: "I don't want to."
O: "Hey, I don't believe what I'm hearing. I can't believe you wouldn't think of your friends—I've never known you to be selfish before."
Y: "I don't want to."
O: "Hey, how about if I pick you up in a half hour—you'll be in the mood by then."
Y: "I don't want to."

The fourth and simplest technique is: Ending the Conversation. Since this one is also most likely to be offensive, it should be used only after other methods have been tried or in desperate situations. The above phone conversation might go like this:
Other: "Come on out for awhile and have a few drinks with us."
You: "Thanks anyway, but I don't want to tonight."
O: "Hey-y-y-y, what's wrong?"
Y: "I just don't want to thanks anyway have fun bye now (click)."

Let's review a little here. The most common forms of manipulation occur when the other person 1) does something that seems to force a decision on you, 2) "convinces" you that what you want to do is unreasonable or dumb, or 3) "convinces" you that you are bad for wanting what you want. With regard to 1), it is normally possible to do what you choose even if the other seems to force a different decision on you. (It is usually even possible to be *nice* while doing it.) For 2) and 3) there are specific verbal techniques that counter manipulative criticism, namely, 1) Asking Objective Questions (how? in what way?) in order to exhaust the criticism; 2) Accepting Criticism, so that it doesn't work; 3) Repeating Yourself (i.e., what you want to do) in a calm voice, instead of dealing at all with criticism; and 4) Ending the Conversation (and just going ahead to do what you choose). These techniques are often effective when used in combination.

Of course, it is your choice whether you want to use any of the above methods. With good friends especially, some of these techniques may seem rude or offensive. And besides, someone may have a good reason for asking you to do something you hadn't planned on doing. But the point is that you can go along with someone else's wishes *or* assert your own instead. It's up to *you*. I'm not telling you to use any of the above methods. But they are there for you *if* you want to use them. (By the way, most assertion therapists suggest that you practice these techniques by role-playing with friends. Have your friend criticize you and try to make you feel guilty, while you practice responding assertively. Not only will you have practice for when the real thing happens, but your anxiety level will be lower too. You see, just knowing what to do isn't doing it. If you feel too anxious when a manipulative situation occurs, you may not go through with your assertive plan. But research has shown that repeated practice in the role-play situation lessens anxiety in the real-life experience.) If you have *really* high anxiety about such situations, don't *force* yourself to confront them. Some of the suggestions in Chapters 10 and 14 may help. Or you may want to consult a counselor.

One more thing about choices of behavior. If you have a good friend, lover, spouse, or other person with whom you have an intimate relationship, some of your time will be taken up in deciding how to meet your wants *and* those of the other person when your wants don't coincide. Of course, you *can* just assert your own will all the time and have other people resent you for it. Or you can let the other person make all the decisions (and then *you* will be resentful). Or you can even compromise, except that in a compromise usually neither person gets exactly what he or she wants—both give up something, and thus may be resentful. A better way is to do some creative thinking and come up with a way to meet both people's wants (and not just partially). For example, suppose you are shy and your friend or spouse is extroverted; and you hate it when you're at a party together where you don't know anyone else and your friend leaves you to fend for yourself. A compromise might entail you and your partner agreeing to alternate—one party your partner spends his or her time with you, and next time you fend for yourself, and so on. But such a compromise isn't all that good for either of you because you'll both resent the fact that you have to give up something every other time. You need a solution that will please both of you. The answer might be not to go to any parties *together* unless you already know some of the people there. That way your partner doesn't have to stick by you all the time and you don't have to fend for yourself.

Or, suppose a friend has a problem that she wants to talk over with you. But you wanted to go out this evening instead. If you say no and go out, you'll probably feel guilty. If you stay home to talk with her, however, you may feel resentful for having to give up something important to you (and you may be distracted all evening thinking of the fun you're missing). With a little creative thought you can come up with a way to satisfy both wants. For example, you could agree to talk with your friend for two hours earlier in the evening and then go out afterwards. "Angie, I've only got till 8:30, but if that's OK, I'd be happy to talk with you." That way you won't feel resentful, the other person won't feel she's burdening you, and you can devote yourself completely to her during the two hours. (More time probably wouldn't help much anyway, since it's not so much the amount of time but the quality of the time spent that makes the difference.)

Isn't life easier when you realize how many choices you have, and you know that other people can't make you do things you don't want (unless you want them to)? After reading this chapter, you are now armed with the tools for doing what you choose. In the next chapter you will learn how Taoism can help you accomplish more by doing less.

Sound interesting? Read on.

10

What Taoism Can Teach You
About
Doing Without Doing

Although it's spelled with a "t," the philosophy we will explore in this chapter is pronounced "Dowism," and its book of scripture is the "Dow-du-jung" (Tao-teh-ching). Lao Tzu, the founder of Taoism, was probably born about 600 B.C.in China. It's interesting to note that he lived at the same time as a number of other great religious leaders throughout the world: Confucius, also from China; Siddhartha Gautama, the Buddha, from India; Zoroaster, from Persia; Socrates, Plato, and Aristotle, from Greece; and the Hebrew prophets, from Israel. In diverse parts of the world, all these great philosophers spoke of love and the basic unity of humanity at the same time, 2,500 years ago.

Unlike what you might expect of a religious leader, Lao Tzu never started a church or went around preaching. As a matter of fact, tradition has it that he only wrote the Tao-teh-ching because a gatekeeper saw him leaving his country and asked him to stay a few days to write down his ideas. The result was a small book of 81 simple but profound poems called the Tao-teh-ching, or "The Way and its Power." After that, Lao Tzu was never heard from again.

There are many interesting ideas in Taoist philosophy, but the one I want to talk about in this chapter is *wu wei*. It sort of means doing something by doing nothing. A style of being passive and yet paradoxically active at the same time. Wu wei is sometimes translated as "creative quietude." This is the way to be in tune with the universe, says the Tao-teh-ching.

Have you ever noticed that sometimes the more you try at something, the more effort you put into it, the more it doesn't work? For example, you're trying to remember something, and it doesn't come to you until you *stop* trying. Or you're trying to be creative, and you can't *make* inspiration come. But when you sit back and relax, it happens. The Taoist concept of wu wei, or accomplishing something by not trying to accomplish something, stands in sharp contrast to the usual Western way of doing things. We often speak of manipulating nature, getting control over the world. We referred to the conquering of Mount Everest. One Oriental writer said, "*We* would have called it the *befriending* of Mount Everest."

You'll recall that in the last chapter I said, "You are now armed with the tools for doing what you choose." Note the military metaphor ("armed"). A Taoist might have put it this way: You are now *un*armed so that you will be free to do what you choose. Interesting difference, eh? Let the tao (the way of the universe, the way of reality) flow within you and through you, says the Tao-teh-ching. Release your acquisitiveness, your desire to take things over. Let the tao flow through you and more will be accomplished than if you set out trying to accomplish it yourself.

The idea here is not really that you go through life being passive. It's just that if you really understand how life works, you won't need to use a lot of force to get things done. Taoists tell the story of a fisherman who was able to catch big fish with only a slender thread because the thread was made so that it had no weak points at which to break. Actually, we in the West have our own fable to illustrate this point. It's the story of the argument between the sun and the wind as to who was the stronger. They agreed that the test of their strength would be a man wearing a cloak—whoever got the cloak off the man would win the contest. The wind blew and blew, but the man merely wrapped his cloak more tightly around himself at each flurry. The sun used no force. He merely warmed the man up so that he voluntarily took his cloak off.

Chuang Tzu, an ancient teacher of Taoism, told the story of a butcher whose cleaver never got dull. His secret was that he always cut in the joints, or spaces *between* the bones, so that he could cut his meat without wearing down his cleaver. Again, the point is, if you know how the universe and life work, you won't need to work so hard to get things done. In fact, if you look carefully, you'll see that often the best way to do *something* is to look for the nothing. The butcher was able to cut his meat so well by looking for the nothingness between the bones, the space between the bones, and aiming there. Look at a cup, and you'll see that it's not the material the cup is made of that's important. It's the space *inside* the material; it's the nothingness inside that holds the liquid. Look at your house. What is it that lets people in and out of it? It's not the door, but the door*way*—the empty space. The door itself just covers up the space when it's not in use.

The best symbol Taoists have for the way of the universe and the way we should live to be in tune with it, is water. Water flows along. If you try to fight it and thrash around in it, you could drown. If you stop fighting it, the water will lift you up and carry you along safely. Notice how water doesn't take over other things. The water flowing in a stream doesn't push things out of its way. It just flows around them, *filling in the empty spaces*. And you know what? Eventually the sharp stones which resisted its flow are worn smooth—they become pebbles. Without force, without pushing, more is changed. "Man at his best is like water," says the Tao-teh-ching. "What is more fluid, more yielding than water? Yet back it comes again, wearing down the tough strength which cannot move to withstand it. So it is that the strong yield to the weak, the proud to the humble. This we know but never learn."

One more thing about water. When it's muddy, the way to

clear it up is not to frantically stir it. Let it stand still and it will clear up by itself. So too with muddy vision. If you want to see clearly, says Taoism, stop looking for awhile. Withdraw from the glare of the world and let yourself see into your soul. In quietness you will see the Way—the way your life must work and the way the universe works.

Much more could be said about this 2500-year-old philosophy, but for our purposes enough has been said about the idea of wu wei, or doing-without-doing, so that it can be applied practically.

One of the earliest applications of wu wei ever developed is judo (from the Japanese "jujitsu," meaning the art of *yielding*), which is a form of physical defense in which you don't attack the other person but rather turn the other's attack into himself. When using this art to defend yourself, you don't need to strike the other person—you merely maneuver in such a way as to let the person's attempt to strike *you*, hit himself.

Since most personal violence in our day is of a psychological nature, I think you'll find *psychological* judo much more useful than the physical kind. Suppose someone attacks you personally. Most people's "automatic" response would be to attack back. But that often does not accomplish anything and it may even make you look pretty bad. Do this instead: Don't attack. Let your opponent make herself look bad by being derogatory. Don't lower yourself to doing the same thing. This will have two effects: It will eventually stop the other's attacks (it's no fun keeping it up if it's not being returned—in fact, the other person will look pretty silly after a while, talking to the air); and you may come off looking better (and ultimately "winning" by *not* trying to win) because your non-response will make it seem that either you are above getting upset by personal criticism, or else you don't consider the criticism at all true. Suppose someone tells you you're a selfish idiot. Responding with "So are you" or "How dare you say that?" is likely to keep the foray going. Saying "I'm sorry you feel that way" or saying nothing at all may be a much better defense (because it's a non-defensive defense).

Let's say a three-year-old told you that you were dumb. How would you look if you started arguing and defending yourself? Pretty foolish, I can tell you. Why? Because everyone knows that an attack from a three-year-old doesn't have the power to put you down. So if you don't argue and defend yourself when an *adult* attacks you, you may make his or her criticism seem like much the same thing—insignificant, inconsequential, even silly, like criticism from a three-year-old.

A friend of mine once told me she thought I was a pretty phoney person. I didn't fight the criticism. I just said, "Yes, I often am. Not everyone else sees it as clearly as you do." What could she say to that? I wasn't resisting her attack. (I wasn't lying either because I *am* often phoney—which is a part of myself I have accepted.) Because of my acceptance of her criticism she was able to express the feeling behind her statement—her fear that I didn't really like her and was "phoney nice" to her—and our relationship was bettered through that honesty.

Another example: I have often written "guest commentaries" for the opinion page of the local newspaper on controversial or unpopular subjects. The responses in the letters-to-the-editor column are usually varied, but I think the ones that have gained the most support for my position have been the letters that were the most personally derogatory. For example, one letter claimed that, by propagating "liberal" views, I posed a graver threat to society than the Boston Strangler and that I was wrecking hearts and homes and civilization itself. An outlandish response like that makes the responder look pretty irrational. You don't need to fight criticism like that—when you do, you make it seem worth fighting against. Let your opponent dig her own grave, so to speak. You will look much better by contrast. In fact, letting others criticize you is often the best boost to your support, especially if those who criticize go overboard and make themselves look foolish. To reverse an old proverb, "With enemies like that, who needs friends!"

Most politicians, by the way, understand this principle quite well. If they are criticized severely, they can usually count on a "backlash" reaction. That is, they can count on others adding their support and counteracting the critics. I understand that former President Nixon's campaign managers used this idea to great advantage. At his rallies there were always a number of protestors who were waiting outside, clamoring for a chance to make their views known. Nixon's managers would let a limited number of them in to some of his rallies, preferably the most obnoxious ones. Then, when they were disruptive or shouted obscenities, Nixon supporters could point to them and say, "*These* are the kind of people who oppose us."

The irony here is that the protestors probably thought they were helping their cause through their actions, when indeed they were assuring its defeat. They had never learned what every good politician knows—the Taoist principle of wu wei—accomplishing something without *doing* anything, meeting aggression with *non*-aggression.

The last shall be first, the first shall be last, the *under*dog wins. Not every time. But a darn good percentage of the time. And most often in the long run.

Look at some of the great humanitarian leaders in our time and through history—for example, Socrates, Jesus, Mahatma Gandhi, and Martin Luther King. Each of them probably accomplished as much through their death as they did through their life. Death is the ultimate state of not-doing, and yet it can sometimes accomplish more than a whole lifetime of words and deeds. Who do you think brings more sympathy and support to an idea or cause—the person who lives comfortably while espousing it...or the one who suffers and dies because of it? Think about the power of unpower, the force of non-force, the strength of life in those who give life up.

Of course, Jesus, Gandhi, and King demonstrated the

power of wu wei in their lives as well as in their deaths. Jesus advocated not resisting force with force or evil with evil, and turning the other cheek, doing good to persecutors, loving enemies. And the non-violent tactics of Martin Luther King and Mahatma Gandhi are among the most potent examples of social-change methods ever witnessed in the 20th century. Imagine protesting segregation by just *sitting* in restaurants and doing *nothing*. Powerful. Very powerful. And how were buses desegregated? Again, by doing a "nothing"—that is, by not riding them. Both King and Gandhi showed the world how to effectively use boycotts. You see, having a boycott isn't *doing* something—it's *not* doing something. It's *not* buying a particular product or patronizing a particular business or organization. And this not-doing can "do" a lot. A strike works on basically the same premise. Want to upset the system? Then don't do anything with it.

Look at the history of the labor movement in the United States if you want to see whether not working works or not. Look at the history of boycotts to see whether you can purchase something worthwhile by not purchasing. Look at life—your own and society's—and know the power there is in non-power, the effect that not doing has on what gets done.

Still another example of forceful non-force is the creative use of silence. Have you ever seen a crowd of people talking and noticed that when a "lull" in the coversation occurs—that is, a gap—suddenly everybody is at attention? When you are continually bombarded with noise, silence makes a dramatic contrast. It is doing-nothing in sound. The next time you are in a group discussion, try a little experiment: Don't say anything for the duration of most of the discussion. Let others do the talking. Then at the end, open your mouth to say a few words. Chances are, everyone will suddenly give you their undivided attention—especially if you speak softly. There is power in not speaking. By saying little, the little you say has more effect.

We discussed techniques for avoiding being manipulated by others in Chapter 9—did you realize that these are practical applications of Taoism too? The technique of Asking Objective Questions when someone criticizes you in order to stop you from doing what you want, is in effect taking a person's use of force or control directed at *you*—and turning it back to the person (*without* sarcasm, bitterness, or aggression). The technique of Accepting Criticism is meeting aggression with non-aggression (because you don't criticize or argue back)—and in effect using a non-power response to deflect attempts to take away your power. Repeating Yourself and Ending the Conversation are also examples of not asserting your strength in order to assert your strength. Quite effective.

Now I'd like to show you how to take wu wei and use it to effect change or reform in any system. Suppose you want to introduce a new concept to a group or institution that is normally not receptive to innovation. If you present or "package" your idea as something that doesn't threaten the system, as something that is indeed *part* of the system, it will meet less resistance (because the idea itself did not resist). Advertisers have recognized this truth for years. When they introduce a product that may seem to go against prevailing values or customs, they often package it with tradition so that it will appear to harmonize rather than resist. That's why some drugs, which could be viewed as threats to good old-fashioned values, are presented with a grandmother or grandfather in the commercial reminding you that it's OK because *they* used it too in the "good old days." Cosmetics for men, which could be viewed as threatening to traditional masculine values, are usually presented as having a "manly" odor or having "strength" for a man (deodorants), or as giving men advantage in sexual attractiveness to women (thus reinforcing the usual male values).

Don't forget the use they've made of the fact that men shave their faces and women don't. How do you get men to agree to buy perfume? Simple. You call it after-*shave* cologne.

What we're talking about here is "flowing through" the

system rather than setting something up to fight and resist it. In the end, this kind of approach often gets more changed in the system than all the direct attempts to alter it. Remember, wu wei is like water, flowing in between the spaces so as not to intrude — but wearing down those tough boulders just the same. Here's a story that I'm told is true, which illustrates the point: Two monks were complaining to each other that they wished they had more recreation periods during the day so that they could smoke. They finally decided to ask their superior if they could have a cigarette during part of the time set aside for prayer. One received permission for this. The other did not and couldn't understand why. "I just asked if I could smoke while I pray," he said. "Oh," said the other. "That's the difference then. I asked if I could pray while I smoked."

Suppose you are an employee of a company that has no vehicle for airing employee complaints, suggestions, and dissatisfactions; and you don't think the management would be particularly receptive to letting workers form a committee for that purpose. Well, trying to get such a group together would be bucking the system and, even if management reluctantly agreed to the idea, they would probably always view the group with suspicion and not be at all eager to carry out its suggestions. So, rather than create resistances here, flow *through* the system instead. Suggest to your employer that it might be a good idea to have a committee to explain management decisions to the workers — a group to smooth over possible conflicts and in general to expedite the company's policies. Naturally, to be effective, the committee should be made up of employees who are respected and trusted by their fellow workers.

Great. Now you have a committee that management won't view as threatening because it's there to help *management — and* you have the committee for airing employee complaints, suggestions, and dissatisfactions. It can do this and do it effectively — after all, it's got the right people on it — and get a more sympathetic hearing from management besides.

Flow through.

And now for another practical application of Taoist philosophy: leaderless leading. The Tao-teh-ching says: "Leaders are best when the people do not know they exist...When the leaders' works are accomplished and their goals achieved, the people will say, 'We did this ourselves.'" That's right. If you want to get something done that needs the help and support of other people, then don't try to lead it all by yourself. Tell the people about whatever situation it is that needs resolving, ask them how they think it should be resolved, and then watch them resolve it. Will it take money to get it accomplished? Don't worry about it. If there are enough people interested, money will be no problem — they'll raise it. *You* don't have to do it in order to get it done. In fact, by *not* doing it you may encourage others to rise up to the challenge.

The way to get others to take on a task that you think is important is to *let them own* the project. Then they will be committed to its importance. Any fund-raiser will tell you this, by the way. If you want the members of your organization to raise money for it, then let them get together to set up the budget. Once they realize what things cost and feel committed because of their part in deciding how to spend it, they will raise the necessary funds. If you want your committee to solve a problem for you, then give them the problem, not the solution. If you give them the solution, then it's *your* answer. If you give them a problem and *they* come up with a solution, then it's *their* answer — and they will be more motivated to implement it. Even if you already have a solution to your problem, you can act as if you don't and present the problem to the group. Some of the ideas they suggest will probably be the same as or similar to (or *better* than) the ones you had in mind anyway, and you can just latch on to those and thank the group for coming up with them. And then watch them implement them. You can bet they'll work harder on them than if they didn't go through that process of participation.

If you want a government program for the needy to succeed, you've got to do the same thing. Don't give them the program from "on high." Get them to do it themselves. When people are asked to run their own program, they get involved in it and make it work. The difference between many programs for the poor that are effective, and those that aren't, is that the effective ones usually had the people who were targeted for help picking their own leaders and deciding the program objectives and ways to implement the objectives.

Many teachers understand the principle of leaderless leading and use it effectively in the classroom. Let's say there's a noise problem. Instead of just yelling at the students to "be quiet," they ask the children to devise rules so that everyone can have a chance to speak. The kids will usually think of rules similar to what the teacher would have given (often their rules are even stricter!) — like, "Only one person talks at a time," "Raise your hand before speaking." But the difference will be that the students have created the rules themselves — and are much more likely to follow them because *they own them.*

Amazing, isn't it? *All* you usually have to do to get things done which need other people's support or participation is to 1) show them that it's something they want to do, and 2) watch them do it. Actually, sometimes people will even do something for you that they *don't* want to do very much, as long as they had a part in planning it. Suppose you go to a person or group and ask for suggestions on how to get publicity for a project or cause you believe in. "I'm not asking for volunteers, because I know all of you are already busy and involved up to your ears," you tell them. "I just want your *ideas.*" OK, now they're relaxed because they don't feel any pressure to do anything except talk. Then you start writing down all their ideas and asking questions about them, like how to do this, how to do that. One of the questions you ask them, by the way, is how to get people to do all these wonderful things they're suggesting, especially how to get *competent* people. Well, if the group gets very involved in the planning, they are going to feel a commitment to the project, even if they weren't all that interested in it in the beginning. If the project seems destined to fail for lack of volunteers, they will feel that they have wasted their time. You can bet at least one of them will volunteer services, if only to keep that investment of time and energy secure.

Without even *asking* for help, you get it—by letting others be the leaders.

Now, if you're ready for still another example of how to use wu wei, here are four words of advice that could eliminate half of the problems in your life. Read this carefully now. The advice I want to give you is simple. But don't dismiss it because of that. It's simple, all right. It's *also* profoundly effective when followed. My advice is this: GIVE UP BEING RIGHT.

You could eliminate perhaps half of your problems by stopping your obsession with being right all the time. Let other people be right instead. If you do that for them, it's amazing what they'll often do for you. (And remember, you haven't actually *done* anything when you let someone else be right—but boy, that not-doing can be pretty effective.)

For example, I have been stopped by the police a number of times for minor traffic violations—not making a complete stop at a stop sign, driving a little over the speed limit, etc. Whenever that happens I let the policeman be right. (He usually is anyway.) Even if I think he's wrong I don't say, "Well, I'm sorry, but you're wrong, Officer." No, in that case I just say, "Gee, Officer, I didn't realize this was illegal." If he gives me a ticket anyway, and I'm right, then I can fight it in court. But if I don't make a point of being the one who's in the right and putting him in the wrong—then he's less likely to give me a ticket. And right or not right, it's worth it to not get a ticket whether I win later in court or not. Even if I *am* right, for the dubious satisfaction of shooting off my mouth I would still have the hassle of going to court.

For all the times I've been stopped and given a warning,

I've never received a ticket. In fact, I want to tell you about one case which was really rather amazing. My car had stalled on an interstate freeway, and a friend of mine came by to help me out. In order to recharge my battery he turned his car on the shoulder to face mine so that we could attach jumper cables. Later a patrolman drove by and, when he saw us, parked behind and then got out to bawl my friend out for illegally parking on the shoulder. He told him he was going to give him a $100 fine and said that not only would *my* car have to be towed away but my friend's would too—because he wasn't going to let my friend make another U-turn on the shoulder. After a few minutes of ranting and raving the policeman went back to his car and waited.

My friend was pretty angry and thought of answering back, but I had a better idea. I went back to the patrolcar and said in my meekest voice (which wasn't difficult to muster because I *felt* meek): "Officer, I feel bad about this—I feel I should get the ticket. My friend came here to help me out, so it's really my fault that this happened, and I feel responsible." The policeman grunted and said again that it was illegal. I told him I agreed and that I felt very responsible.

And you know what happened? Not only did my friend not get a ticket—but the policeman let him make a U-turn on the shoulder so that we could drive back!

Afterwards, in discussing what had happened, my friend told me he would have argued right back instead of handling it the way I did. If he had, he would have gotten the satisfaction of "being right." Only, the satisfaction would probably have cost him $100 plus towing.

I was glad to take the $100 over being right! That *doesn't* mean I'd compromise my *principles* for $100. It does mean I've come to value other people—and their opinions—as *equal* to me and mine.

There are countless examples from your own life—past, present, and future—in which giving up being right (and letting someone else be right instead) gets you more. Next time you want to get a co-worker to help you out on something, which approach do you think will get you the cooperation you need: "Come on, you're not doing that much anyway, so help me out" (you're right, the other is wrong)—or, "I know you're really busy, so I'll understand if you can't help, but I'd really appreciate it if you could" (they're in the right, and you let them be there)?

Next time you're in an argument over something that you don't even care that much about, stop the debate by saying: "Listen, I don't even know why I'm arguing about this. I'm sorry I've been giving you such a rough time." The *other* person may even back down and say, "Yeah, well, I didn't mean to get so extreme on this myself. Sorry about that." I remember a woman who came in to talk about a letter she found, addressed to her teenage daughter, which revealed some serious problems that the mother felt she had to talk to her daughter about. But she didn't know how to bring the problems up without making her daughter defensive and angry that her mother had read her mail. I gave the mother this advice: Approach your daughter by putting *yourself* in the wrong (which was honest—it probably *was* wrong to invade her daughter's privacy). Tell her you apologize for having read her mail—"I know I shouldn't have read it and I apologize; but I still feel we should discuss it."

Well, she used this approach and it worked. Her daughter opened up, because she wasn't put on the defensive.

Such a simple thing. When you insist on being right, others react defensively. When you let other people be right instead, it's incredible to see what they'll do for you in return. You don't always have to fight to get what you want. You don't have to raise yourself up or your ideas up. (If you do, you invite others to raise *them*selves up to resist you.) Don't always set up something to resist others. Be like water. You may not look like you're doing much, but when things start to gently float down your way you'll understand the smooth power of water—it's so flexible that it overcomes resistances without seeming to. Which is exactly what you can do if you give up being right.

A corollary to this method, by the way, is to be critical of yourself—*before* other people get a chance to be. That is, when you make a mistake or botch things up, publicly admit it. That way it will be harder for people to put you down. They won't *want* to, if you are already admitting your mistake. People normally only want to bring people down who they think are too high. If you bring yourself down, they won't have the need to do it for you. I know the director of an organization who used this method quite effectively. When he did something that could draw criticism, he disarmed his would-be criticizers (disarm = take weapons away— interesting military metaphor, don't you think?) by saying something like this: "I want to apologize for not handling this properly. I didn't do it right, and you've got a right to be critical of me on this."

What could they say to that?

You will find this easier to do once you increase your self-esteem (see Chapter 16 for some help with that) so that you won't feel the need to always look good. You won't mind admitting your shortcomings—and you'll make it easier to work with people.

Let's review now the practical applications of wu wei, or doing without doing, that we've noted so far:

1) "psychological" judo (in which you let the other person's attack against you make the other look bad, by simply not responding or at least not attacking);
2) strikes, boycotts, and other forms of non-resistance;
3) silence;
4) counter-manipulation techniques (see Chapter 9);
5) "flowing through" the system;
6) leaderless leading;
7) giving up being right; and
8) being critical of yourself and "disarming" potential attackers.

There. You've got eight practical examples of doing without doing. And you can think of more. You know how? Without *trying*. Just let them come to you. That's how I wrote this chapter. I just let the ideas come. I didn't have to do anything to make them come. (But I combined this not-doing with doing. Here's how: Everytime an idea "came" to me, I wrote it down on one of those slips of paper that I carry around with me. You see, doing and doing-by-not-doing are not antithetical to each other—rather, they make an effective team when used together!)

Give yourself a week, and I'll bet you will come up with at least two new ways to apply wu wei to your living. And the ideas will come to you without your trying to make them come. And without your doing anything to have them come. Just slow down and let it happen. There's a lot inside you that could help you, if you would just give it a chance to surface.

Now, as much as I wish it weren't so, doing-without-doing can be used in destructive ways too. Passive aggression is one example of this. (Interesting combination of words— "passive" and "aggressive"—two opposites, one denoting acting or doing, the other denoting *in*action.) Passive aggressive people try to make you angry by not saying or doing anything—they've learned how effective that is in getting their way.

The "powerless" martyr is another example of manipulating others by *pretending* to not be able to do anything. It's amazing what such manipulators accomplish (by getting others to do everything for them) despite their "health condition" and seeming powerlessness.

The self put-down is still another example of manipulating others—in this case, getting them to give us praise because we are afraid to praise ourselves. We say something bad about ourselves (like "I'm dumb" or "I'm ugly") so that others will jump in and say, "Oh, you're not dumb (bad/ugly/boring, etc)." Although our strategy usually works, we never know whether the other person really meant the compliment or was just trying to make us feel good.

Besides, for the gift of praise we had to lower ourself, and that takes a toll on our self-esteem.

It would be nice if people did not use wu wei in destructive ways like this, but people can and people do. That's just the way it is. I can hope that people reading this book will use what I've said only in constructive ways. But hoping doesn't get me anything. Ultimately it's up to you how you use *any*thing I say here.

You know, if you really got deeply into the Taoist way of life, you probably wouldn't even think of using the principle of accomplishing-without-doing for such mundane things as looking good or getting out of paying traffic fines. Having things and doing things would no longer be so important to you. In fact, *things* wouldn't be very important to you, period.

But that's probably not where you and I are at right now. No use pretending we are. Just accept whatever level you're at. If your life is pretty shallow or superficial, so what? Admit it. The people who recognize how shallow they are, are already deeper than most of the people who claim to be deep. It takes at least some depth to see your superficiality.

And the neat thing about Taoism is that you can use it at a shallow level or at a deep level or anywhere in between. You don't need to apologize to anyone for not being a mystic or a guru. Just be where you are and accept it. (You can't move beyond where you are unless you acknowledge it anyway, because that's the way "enlightenment" happens.)

If, however, you think you would like to become more detached from the maddening rush of things, then try the following exercise, which has been variously called meditation, autosuggestion, self-hypnosis, centering oneself, prayer, body shut-down, relaxed awareness. It's merely stopping yourself, or unwinding, and in its basic thrust fits nicely with Taoism (and Buddhism and Hinduism — actually with *any* lifestyle). In order to see, sometimes you have to stop looking. This relaxation exercise enables you to do that — to stop, period.

Read the following paragraphs over slowly several times so that you can say them to yourself without reading — or else say them out loud slowly into a tape recorder and then play the tape back while you follow the instructions.

Ready? Here it is:

Sit down in a chair. Don't slouch — sit up with your back firm against the back of the chair and your feet flat on the floor, but be relaxed. Let your hands rest on your legs. (If you like, let your palms face up with fingers restfully pointing upwards, to symbolize receptivity to all that may ''come'' to you.)

Close your eyes. Good. Let your awareness be on your feet. Let all the tension out of them, first from your toes and then from your whole feet. Let them feel very, very relaxed, as if pounds and pounds of tension and energy are just flowing out of them. Let it all pour out. (pause)

Good. Now let the energy stored in the calves of your legs out too. Just let it out. Relax those muscles. Let them feel calm...peaceful...at rest. (pause)

Fine. Now let this restfulness come up to your knees. Let all the tension out, from the top of your knees to your toes. Let it *all* out. Let it drain. (pause)

Now be aware of your thighs. Feel the tension in them...Now feel the tension going away. It's leaving. Just let it go. Just let it gradually evaporate and leave your thighs feeling light. (pause)

Feel the energy in your hips and your groin area. Let that out. Let all the activity, the uneasiness, the heaviness — let it drain out of you. That's right. Just let it go and leave you relaxed, free. (pause)

Good. Now be aware of your stomach. There's probably a good deal of tension in your stomach muscles. Release it. Release it all. Let all that tension out of your stomach. Feel it pouring, draining, disappearing. Your stomach will feel very relaxed and calm. (pause)

Now let your awareness be on the area above your stomach, including your chest. There's stored-up energy there—tensions and anxieties. Let them go. Just let them roll out and away. Feel them gradually drain away, leaving you with a light and peaceful feeling. (pause)

Good. Now feel your back and shoulders. Experience the tensions there as so many knots of frenzied activity. Untie the knots. That's right. Untie all those knots, one at a time...Keep untying them, and as you do, let the bound-up energy be free to drain away. Go ahead and let that tension out. (pause)

Now, your hands and arms. Your hands have been moving around all day, lifting, gesturing. Those fingers have been grabbing, clutching. Your arms holding, moving. Make fists with your hands, then tighten up those arm muscles. Hold it tight. Hold it. Keep on holding those muscles tight. A little bit longer. ...There. Now relax them and just feel *all* that tension leave. Your arms and hands don't have to do anything now. Just let them relax on your legs and feel the good feeling of every last ounce of tension draining away and leaving you with a marvelous feeling of peace. Very peaceful. Very relaxed. Very calm. (pause)

Good. Now focus your awareness on your neck. Relax all those neck muscles. Relax them so much that you can feel a state of peace flowing from your neck down through your *whole* body. That's right. Just let all that tension run out. Take some time for this. (longer pause)

Good. Now let out all the pains and tensions in your head. Relax your jaws; let your eyes rest; let your forehead be relaxed. Be aware of the spaces between your eyebrows and right above them—let the tension flow out of this area. Relax your ears, your mouth, your nose, your scalp. Just let all the anxiety and frenzied energy drain away from your head so that your entire body, from head to toe, feels utterly peaceful and calm. You are relaxed, at rest, feeling light. (pause)

Fine. Now I'd like you to stay in this state of relaxed awareness for about ten or fifteen minutes.

You don't have to think about anything. Shut out all the worries and concerns of the day. If you find yourself getting distracted or your mind wandering,...just acknowledge whatever it is you're thinking about and then let it slip away. (If you like, be aware of your breathing—in and out...in and out. Breathe in with me now, and let it feel like a wave coming in from a sandy shore, refreshing you. ...Now let your air out slowly and feel the wave receding and opening up an incredibly blue sky for you. That's it. Keep it up.)

Just drink in whatever the universe and you have to offer you, by letting yourself be detached from all those things that fill you up and don't allow you to be empty enough to receive. Be utterly empty. In that way you will be utterly full. (ten- or fifteen-minute pause)

Let yourself gradually return now to the outer world. As I slowly count to ten, I want you to gradually come back to normal awareness. When I reach three, begin to visualize what the room you are in looks like. When I reach seven, slowly open your eyes and become accustomed to the room. By the time I reach ten you should feel at home in the room and relaxed and refreshed, as from a pleasant vacation. One ... two ... three ... four ... five ... six ... seven ... eight ... nine ... ten.

* * * * * * * * * * * * * * *

Variations

1. *Meditation*. The above relaxation exercise is sometimes called meditation, only some people silently or audibly chant a "mantra" (a combination of syllables, like "nogen" or "imtan") over and over, to help keep themselves from being distracted by thoughts or outside events. (Concentrating on your breathing does this for you too.) You can make this exercise as exotic as you like too (in a warm whirlpool bath or

hot tub with incense?).

Most people who practice "meditation" frequently (say, twice a day, for twenty minutes) report that they feel more energy during the rest of the day, their emotions don't erupt as easily, and in general things do not "bother" them as much.

2. *Expanding Consciousness.* You can use the relaxation exercise as a means of helping you broaden your awareness of yourself as part of a larger whole. After you've gotten to the point of total-body relaxation, say these words to yourself (via tape or your own thoughts).

Imagine yourself by yourself. You are you, completely set apart from every other living and nonliving thing. You are just your body. Unique. Alone. (pause)

Now let your awareness include the room you are in (and the people in it, if any) without opening your eyes to see this. This room is all you would be able to see if you opened your eyes. So this room is all there is to your world. You and the room are part of each other—in fact, you *are* the whole room. Let yourself be the room. (pause)

The room you are in is part of a building. Experience that—see the other rooms and the total structure, and let the whole building be your awareness. Just the building. ...Just as you often think of your head, arms, legs, as your body, think now of the building as your body. It is you—you are now the entire building. (pause)

The building you are in is only one among many structures. Let your awareness expand to include the buildings or structures in one geographical area—this city block. Think of this whole block, and let yourself be it. (pause)

Now open your boundaries to a much larger area—this whole city or county. Think of all the people and things in this area. Think of all the things going on and the activities that people are engaged in. You are all of that. Be it. (pause)

Expand. Expand again. You are now an entire state.

Imagine all the people and things and activities...and then be them. (pause)

Open your boundaries now as they've never been opened before. Be the whole country. That's right. Look at the variety in geography, custom, accent, color. ...Enjoy all of that, and then recognize that all of it is you, because you are an American, and you are all of it. Let yourself be it. What a fantastic feeling! (pause)

Now I want you to be aware of the waters surrounding your boundaries. Look at the waves and the broad expanse of oceans spreading out beyond you. Only, instead of letting it be beyond you, go with it and spread out yourself to see other countries, other continents, other peoples. Spread out throughout the whole globe until you meet yourself, east and west, coming and going. Be aware of the entire earth. More than be aware, be *it*. You are the earth. Feel complete and whole as a world, a whole planet. (pause)

You are the earth, a beautiful blue planet hurtling through space at an incredible speed. And you see other worlds—a moon, comets, rocks, asteroids, dust, planets, a fiery ball of sun. These are all a part of you too. Let yourself expand to be the solar system, with your many parts moving and spinning, but all of it part of a oneness, all of it you. (pause)

Now let your awareness skip to the stars. Dash on from orb to fiery orb, dancing through the galaxy Milky Way. Giant globes of fire, planets, explosions—all of it moving, swirling. You race through to explore, only to discover that you are exploring you, for all of this is you too. Be filled with it all. (pause)

Be filled with more. Be now all the stars and galaxies. Be the universe and all that is beyond it. *You* are all that is. All that is, is you. Infinitely complex, infinitely intricate, and all of it is you. You have stretched out to be all—so far and so inclusively that you are no longer separate, no longer an individual entity. You are nothing and everything, nowhere and everywhere. You are all of it. Enjoy that. And just be it. (long pause)

Now gradually, slowly, take yourself back, step by step, through galaxies, through planets and continents and cities, back to the self within the room. Enjoy the journey back. (pause)

As I slowly count to ten you will gradually experience yourself back in this room and open your eyes. But no longer confined, you will now be as large as the universe, as small as an electron. One ... two ... three ... four ... five ... six ... seven ... eight ... nine ...ten.

This consciousness expansion can be done in reverse, by the way. You can become smaller and smaller until you become the smallest particle of an electron. This too is "expansion" in the sense that you are expanding beyond the usual limits you set for your consciousness.

Naturally, consciousness expanding is not an intellectual, but an *experiential* exercise. So it doesn't really matter whether it "makes sense" intellectually to *be* the universe or anything else. However, if the intellectual part is getting in the way of the experience for you, then I'd like you to consider a few "intellectual" details for a few moments.

You are probably used to thinking of "you" as being located inside your body, right? Everything under your skin is you, and everything outside of your skin is not—at least that's the way most people conceive of themselves. But I want you to question that. I mean, are you really *in* your arm, for example? Sure, you seem to *feel* things in your arm, but actually it's your brain that gives you those sensations. If your arm didn't have nerves connecting it with your brain, you wouldn't feel anything in that arm. So it's not really the arm that's feeling anything—it's your brain. The arm makes it possible for your brain to receive feeling messages, but "you" aren't located inside your arm because the arm in itself doesn't feel anything. You are not located in your legs or stomach either. When things happen to these parts of the body, the nervous system sends messages to the brain, but the legs and stomach aren't *having* the sensations. The brain is.

But wait a minute. The *brain* isn't having them either. *You* are. But where are you located? In your brain? No, the brain just makes it possible for you to have thoughts and sensations. *It* is not you.

So *where* are you? "You" are in no particular place at all. (Which is about the same as being everywhere!)

But let's say for a moment that you don't accept that. So we'll look at this from another angle. Suppose you believe your body is you because it makes your feelings and sensations possible. But the environment *surrounding* your body makes all those sensations your body communicates possible too. So it's just as reasonable to say that your *environment* is you as to say your *body* is you. But the *outer* environment makes your *immediate* environment possible, so you could say *that* is you too. So, if you think your body is you, you've got to admit that the universe which makes the body possible is you too. You're everywhere and nowhere — that is, you are in no *particular* place.

Think about that for awhile. If it doesn't make sense right now, just sit with it. It may make sense later on.

And then again, it may not.

And that's OK.

3. *Success Orientation.* The relaxation exercise can be used to "program" yourself for success. Do you have a difficult task to accomplish? Then go into shut-down (relaxed awareness) and imagine yourself in your difficult situation — and imagine yourself handling it well. Imagine your whole day going well — even when difficult outside things come up, imagine yourself handling them with ease and confidence.

This kind of programming (sometimes called auto-suggestion or self-hypnosis) actually makes it easier to achieve the success that you've "dropped" into your "unconscious" (or whatever you want to call that part of your "mind").

4. *Increasing Self-Esteem.* In much the same way as above, you can increase your liking of yourself by saying these words to yourself (or something similar) after getting yourself into a relaxed state:

> I am a unique person. No one else is quite like me. There are others who have this or that quality like mine, but no one whose combination of qualities and talents adds up to exactly what I am.
> I am a loving person. I have done things to help others. I'll think about all those for a few moments.
> I have a sense of humor, even about myself. I'll remember those times now. ...
> I am intelligent and I am talented in many areas, for example...(elaborate).
> I am competent in...(elaborate—think of all those areas).
> Even aside from all these "things" about me, I am myself, and that's enough. In fact, it's more than enough. It's fantastic!

By the way, don't try to pretend that you can't think of anything good to say about yourself. That's a little game we so often like to play. It's self-pitying drivel. Nonsense. A lie. Don't play that game unless you want to stay stuck in your rut.

5. *Getting to Sleep and Waking Up Refreshed.* Do you have trouble getting to sleep at night? Use the relaxation exercise to help you get drowsy and fall asleep.

If you would also like to wake up refreshed in the morning, then use this technique, and when you have totally relaxed your body, imagine a clock. Think of whatever time it is at that moment and imagine the hands of the clock moving until they are at the time that you want to get up. Then imagine yourself waking up and feeling completely refreshed.

Do this three times. Also, set your mechanical/electric

alarm clock for ten minutes after your "psychic" alarm clock, just in case. But you'll probably find that, at least after a few trials, your psychic alarm clock will get you up right on time, and you'll feel rested when you get up.

Don't bother with this exercise, by the way, if you don't really *want* to wake up feeling refreshed. (I for one often like to hold the sleep with me for awhile—I even enjoy being grumpy in the morning.) If you *do* want it, then you can make it happen. It's amazing what power you have over your body, even to the point of waking it up "on the button." You didn't realize that because you probably haven't exercised your power before.

6. *Getting in Touch with Your Feelings.* By putting your body into shut-down through relaxed awareness you erode some of the blocks and barriers that you normally put up (unconsciously) to keep unpleasant thoughts away. If you want to know some of your *real* feelings, then relax yourself through the exercise and imagine whoever (or whatever) you are interested in understanding your feelings about. The feelings, when uninhibited in this way, are more likely to surface. In fact, this is a great way to uncover feelings from the past that you may have never worked out. Get into relaxed awareness and as you do so, if there are feelings associated with the various parts of your body (because of past experiences), then let yourself experience them as you go through the exercise with each part of your body. Or, think of the significant people and events of your life and let the feelings you have toward them come out, so that they won't plague you as much in the future.

7. *Desensitization to Problem Emotions.* Behavior modification therapists popularized the gradual desensitization technique in the early 1950s. The idea was to condition fear or anger *out* of you by conditioning *in* a feeling that is incompatible with those—namely, a calm, relaxed state. Although the theoretical basis for this technique has recently

been seriously questioned, the technique itself appears to be rather effective. You get yourself into the relaxed state with the relaxation exercise and then you imagine the situations that normally arouse fear or anger. Through repeated imaginings you eventually reduce the fear or anger response. However, in order to be effective, the desensitization should be gradual—that is, you should start with only mild fear- or anger-provoking situations and work your way up.

I will explain the details for using this technique in Chapter 13 (which deals with problem feelings).

8. *A Fun Place to Go to.* Do you want a vacation? A nice place to visit when things are hectic and you want to relax? Here's a way to get this without spending a cent. Just relax through the exercise and imagine some scene that is particularly pleasing to you—one you've actually seen before or one created completely by you. It might be a beach, with you lying in the sand and letting the cool waves of water roll in to refresh and tingle you. Or you can be running along the beach feeling the exhilaration of moving with the wind.

How about a meadow scene, with sun and shade, beautiful and fragrant flowers, with or without lake or river? Or perhaps you would like a totally new experience for your "place": another planet, flying through the clouds, or a house you build yourself (design it and even go through the motions of constructing it and hammering it together—this will help cement it in your mind as your own personal "center").

It's free—both in terms of not costing you any money and in being *whatever* you want it to be. Your own place of fantasy. Enjoy it!

* * * * * * * * * * * * * *

There's so much to have and be and accomplish—without doing anything to get there. That's the message of this chapter. I've given you examples. But your own life can be the best example of doing without doing. Go ahead. Your life-example will be different from mine. Unique. Because you're unique.

And that's neat.

11

Working with the Chips
You Have

You only have a certain amount of them, you know. Chips.
In the last several chapters you've been learning about how
to decide what you want, how to get things done that you put
off, getting beyond trying and hoping, managing what you
want despite others' attempts to manipulate you, and
accomplishing things without doing much. Now I want to
remind you that there is only a limited amount of chips
available to you. As I said in Part One, there are many things
you can't do, and so you might as well get used to the idea.
(You can't change your age or your I.Q. And you can't change
the law of gravity. You've got to walk with it. Oh, I know, it
would be nice to just fly around, sans airplane, but that's not
the way it is. So enjoy walking!)
You see, life is a game. I'm sure you've heard that analogy
before. But now I want you to really see that. Life is a game
where every person gets a certain number of chips. But
they're not equally distributed. You have more chips than
some people and less than others. That's just the way it is. It
does no good to belly-ache over the unfairness of it all. It's
like starting out a board game. People throw the dice.
Someone gets a twelve. Maybe you only get a three. Too bad.
But you can *still* play a good game, even if you start with a
three. You can play a good game no matter what kind of chips
life gives you.
Now, part of the life game is skill, and part of it is just luck.

So you toss your dice and, no matter what you get, you do the best you can with it. And you know, the most important thing isn't so much how many chips you end up with—it's how much you increased your original supply. Suppose you start out with five chips and increase your supply to forty. Suppose someone else starts out with fifty and increases it to fifty-five (or even *decreases* it to forty-five). The other person ends up with more chips than you have. But who do you think played a better game—and had more fun playing it? You, of course. I don't care what you're starting out with right now (by the way, every moment can be seen as a new beginning, if you want)—you can still play a darn good game.

OK. Now I want you to get something else: Play with the chips you have. Don't try to play with chips you don't have. Hardly seems worth making a point about, but so many people do try to play their game with nonexistent chips. Can you imagine how silly it would be if you were playing poker and you started betting with imaginary chips? "There, I'll match your bet and raise you five." "But you're not putting any chips down." "Yeah, that's because I don't have any left, but that's OK—I still want to raise your bet." Crazy. The game has to stop because you're not playing it anymore—you're just taking up time.

You've got to play a game by the rules—by *some* rules, anyway—or it isn't a game. You can only use the chips you have—and betting when you've got nothing to bet with is just silly. Why waste time playing with chips that aren't there?

A woman who once came to me for counseling had a problem with her brother. She was living with her family and needed quiet in order to study for school, but her brother liked to play his stereo loudly and apparently wasn't amenable to compromise. "What can I do about this?" she asked. "He just won't cooperate. Am I being unreasonable?" I told the young woman that I didn't think she was being unreasonable in asking her brother to turn the volume down, but that whether she was being unreasonable or not didn't make a whole lot of difference. I explained to her that life is a game and that one of the chips she *didn't* have was a quiet house to study in. But did that mean life was over? No. She could still play a good game by studying at school or at the public library or at a friend's house. Arguing with her brother about how unreasonable he is—which she had been doing for a long time—just didn't accomplish anything. To continue doing it would be to play a poor game. (Unless, of course, her game was to fight with her brother—in which case she was playing quite well but not being honest about what the game was.)

No matter how few chips you have, you always have *some*, and you can always *do* something with them. "But I want to go to Hawaii for my vacation and I don't have enough money." OK then, Hawaii just isn't one of your chips. Choose from among the ones you have. "But I want Hawaii." Yeah, well, unless you can think of a way to get there you're just wasting time in your game—like the person who stalls everything by betting without poker chips. The game stops for awhile and you don't move ahead at all. You can't until you agree to play again.

Another example. A friend of mine told me she wanted to play the piano in front of an audience, but she was too nervous. She wanted to know what to do about her "problem." She had only two choices (or at least she *believed* she had only two choices, which is the same thing as far as her perspective goes). Her choices were: 1) play the piano in front of people while nervous and perhaps not play well; or 2) not play the piano in front of people. Those were her chips. Performing *calmly* to an audience was a chip she apparently didn't have at this point. So why try to play with it? It just wastes time and creates "problems." (Such nervousness *can* be overcome by a procedure such as the desensitization I'll describe in Chapter 14. But she still didn't have that chip at that time!)

You see, there wasn't really any problem in her situation. She just had two alternatives to choose from. No more problem there than in the law of gravity. You have two

alternatives with gravity too. You can walk with it. Or you can
sit down. But you don't have alternative no. 3: flying with it.
Now, you can make that into a problem: "Oh my God, what
am I going to do? I want to fly and gravity won't let me." But
that would be pretty silly (although no sillier than trying to
play with any other chip you don't have).

Another friend of mine, who was a teacher, complained
that she just couldn't do a good job teaching her class of
children with learning disabilities—unless she took more
time away from doing other things she enjoyed, such as
activities with her family. "Well then," I said, "why don't
you settle for doing a mediocre job at teaching?" "No, I
would find that very unfulfilling and unsatisfactory," she
said, after she thought for a moment. "Irresponsible too."

"Then apparently you can't do both, so what will it be?" I
asked. "But I want to do both," she said. "You want to and
you can't. That's just the way it is. Doing both is a
nonexistent chip in this game. Why waste time trying to play
with it?"

She decided to take the extra time to do a good job teaching
and skip some enjoyable family activities because—and get
this—she wanted to be a responsible teacher *more* than she
wanted to spend extra time with her family. As soon as she
gave up trying to play with the chip she didn't have she was
able to get on with her game.

A personal example: Recently my backpack was stolen
from my car. In it were my only copies of five chapters to this
book, including the one you're reading now. That was hours
and hours of work down the drian. If I wanted, I could really
pour out the details here and make a tear jerker out of this
story. But I'll spare you that and just tell you that I was pretty
depressed about this, as you might imagine. But life does go
on, you know. And you have to keep on playing—with
whatever chips you get. One of the chips I didn't have was a
backpack with five chapters. So I worked with the chips that
were available to me—namely, my memory, my creativity,
and my desire to finish this book. I even learned a few good

things from my mishap. I learned that this book was important to me (because I didn't want to give up writing it); I learned that it's pretty dumb to leave your only copy of something in a place where it can be lost or taken; and I learned that I am capable of bouncing back and rising above adversity.

You might even say I gained a few chips in my game.

You know, there have to be *some* obstacles to make a game interesting. Otherwise it's not much fun. Why do people enjoy chess? Because it's hard to play, of course. There are obstacles, set-backs, that make the game challenging. Try playing checkers with a five-year-old sometime. Not all that exciting, is it. It's so easy it's boring.

Well, life is a game with obstacles to keep it interesting. You won't like all of the obstacles. But you can overcome them and feel good about that, just the same. Losing five chapters to this book wasn't exactly the kind of obstacle I would have chosen to add zest to my life. But my dice came up with a three, as it were, and I dealt with that in the most constructive way I could. The game goes on. I didn't choose all the rules. I didn't choose my chips. I didn't choose the way the dice would come up. But I did choose (and I do choose) to play, and to play well.

By the way, your only choices in the life game are to play well or to play poorly. You don't get to choose not to play. You see, if you were playing Monopoly, you could choose to quit. "Oh no, someone else bought Boardwalk, and I wanted it so badly. So I quit." Yes, you can do that. You can quit the game if you don't like it. But you know what? Your choice to quit is also a choice not to win. Once you're out of the game you lose your opportunity to succeed at the game. In a way, then, quitting a game — even Monopoly — is merely a *decision in advance to lose.*

And that's the way it is in life. You decide not to play anymore, and you lose. So even "quitting" isn't really getting out of the game — because the life game is always going on in one form or another, no matter what you do —

"quitting" is just deciding in advance not to win.

And why do that?

Another by-the-way: In case you think I'm encouraging you to compete with other people in your game, I'm not. If you want to compete, that's fine—then that's part of *your* game. But not everyone is playing the same game as you are. The chips are different for different people. Some people play for money. Some play for prestige. Some play for getting love, others for giving it. Some play for improving the lot of humanity, and still others for security or status or respect or for a combination of things. Don't worry about competing with someone else. The important thing is not how many chips you end up with anyway, or how many more you have than somebody else. It's how much you're increasing your original supply and how much fun you're having in the process. Besides, the game you're playing may be quite different from that played by others. If you've got forty chips in love and only ten in money, and someone else has forty chips in money and only ten in love—then who's *winning*? It all depends on what your game is. You're playing quite well in love. Not so well in money. Whether you consider that "winning" or not depends on which of these you made your jackpot.

You can win. Just decide what it is you want to play for and play with the chips you get. No need to complain that you rolled a three instead of a twelve. No need to compete with anybody else. No need to waste time planning for chips you don't have and won't get. Just play, and play well. For yourself. There's no one else you have to play for. There's no one else to mark down your score and tell you you lost. After all, who else would know whether you're really winning or losing? Only you know what game you're playing. And only you can win it.

12

Trusting and Tuning-Up Your Body

This chapter is about you and your body. I'm not going to promise *perfect* health for you in this chapter. I *am* going to suggest some things which, if you haven't been doing, can make your health *better*. And remember, the real fun in the life-game lies not necessarily in having all the chips there are — but in increasing your original supply of them. (The chips in this case are "wellness" chips.) You may not want to use all the suggestions I give here — and that's OK! I think being healthy has some obvious benefits that far outweigh the "hardship" of obtaining them. But you may not agree! And since only you can judge what is best for you (since only you know what game you're playing), then *you* must make the decisions regarding your health. As I've insisted before, please don't do anything for me. Do it for you. You're the one who will become healthier by following the advice you read here — not anyone else. Decide now whether that's what you want. And if it is, then read it and *do* it!

"Wellness." A number of health leaders are using a new word. For a long time the health profession treated people only after they got sick — they didn't worry about the people who seemed to function all right. Only problem was: A lot of people who got sick might *not* have gotten sick if they had received preventive treatment earlier. Wellness is all about 1) helping already well people get better (even *more* "well"),

and 2) helping already well people keep from getting diseases or other problems later on. If we could do more for people who are OK today, we'd have less not-OK people tomorrow to work on. Health professionals have been so busy putting band-aids on the un-well that they often haven't gotten around to eliminating some of the causes of un-wellness. *You* can save yourself problems tomorrow (*and* live more fully today) by doing some things for your own health. What I'm talking about is usually called preventive health care (that is, health care now that prevents health problems later). But the word "preventive" gives this a negative connotation—viz., we're preventing something negative from happening in the future. *I* prefer to think of wellness as a positive thing—living with more zest, more good physical feelings, more aliveness *today*. The prevention of future illness is merely a nice by-product. For example, if you are a smoker, then giving that up will help to prevent future cancer, loss of hearing, loss of sight, wrinkling of skin, heart attack, etc. But those are only the by-products. What non-smoking gives you *today* is more enjoyment of eating, fewer present health problems (allergies, asthma, bronchitis, high blood pressure), more sensual awareness generally, and more "intouchness" with your feelings.

I'd like to also mention another new word that's being used by leaders in the health field today: "holistic" (or, as it's sometimes spelled, "wholistic"). Holistic health concerns the *whole* person. You see, in the past (and even today) medical doctors often treated only the body, when psychological factors may have been influencing how the body was acting—causing ulcers, headaches, skin problems—which mere physical/medical treatment alone will not solve (it will only change the symptoms). And psychologists have treated psychological problems, presuming that they were only caused by relationships or problems in the family, environment, or other "psychological" or social factors—when often there were underlying physical causes (like obesity, improper nutrition, or other health problems).

Even clergy have treated so-called spiritual problems as if they had nothing to do with psychological feelings or physical difficulties.

The truth is, people are *whole* people. They are not just mind, body, and "spirit"—each going its separate way. My physical health influences how I deal with my emotions and other psychological matters. My emotional ("psychological") health influences how I physically feel (how fast I will recover from physical pains and illnesses). And my sense of personal meaning or fulfillment in life (my "spiritual" side) will influence—and be influenced by—both my physical and psychological health. All three interlock. Actually, the words "physical," "psychological," and "spiritual" (or "existential") are just convenient labels anyway. The more basic truth is that we are whole people—manifesting ourselves in ways that can be conveniently classified in this or that category, but essentially interlocking, interweaving beings.

If you want to continue to grow—older, wiser, and better—for a long time, and to enjoy life more during that time, then here are some suggestions for *holistic wellness*:

1) If you smoke, either stop or cut down. One half to one pack a day may take away 3 years from your life. One or two packs a day can subtract 6 years. And smoking 2 packs or more a day may take away *8 years* of your life!* 2) If you're overweight, change your eating patterns. If you are presently 10 to 30 pounds overweight, then getting back to normal may add 2 years to your life. If you're 30 to 50 pounds over, reducing can give you 4 years. And if you're more than 50 pounds overweight, getting down to normal may save you 8 years of your life!

Besides not smoking and keeping your weight normal, here are some other suggestions for living better and longer from the National Center for Health Services Research and Development: 3) Get enough sleep (for most of us that's 7 or

---

*These and the immediately following statistics are drawn from Shirley Linde's *The Whole Health Catalogue* (see Suggestions for Further Reading), p. 11.

8 hours a night), 4) eat breakfast, 5) don't make a habit of eating between meals, 6) drink alcohol in moderation (or not at all), and 7) exercise frequently.

A few more suggestions for better and longer living: 8) If your blood pressure is high, lower it (through doctor-prescribed medication and/or exercise, plus no salt, no sugar, no licorice, no smoking—or at least drastically reduce these); 9) make sure you get enough vitamins and minerals (through your food or through supplements); 10) cut down on high-cholesterol foods (reduce the amount of fat you eat); 11) cut down on salt; 12) cut down on sugar; 13) if you fly off the handle in stress situations, learn to reduce that too (see how, below); 14) eat more fresh foods and less processed and preserved foods; 15) cut down or eliminate caffeine from your diet (coffee, cola, tea, cocoa, and headache tablets that contain caffeine)—too much can cause anxiety and other health problems.

Now, that's a lot of suggestions! Pick the ones you want to use (if any). And if you'd like practical help in achieving these ends, read on.

Eating, Drinking, Smoking, and Other Addictions: We all have habits which tend to be tough on our wellness. A lot of us are either fat or at least a little overweight. Maybe you drink too much coffee. Or perhaps you would like to quit smoking. Do you have an alcohol problem, or use other drugs more than you would like to? Such habits can really get in the way of health in the holistic sense I'm advocating. In fact, I'd be surprised if you haven't already tried some ways to decrease your eating/smoking/drinking/pill popping behavior!

Let me share with you some methods which have proved effective for dealing with these problems. Not all of them will be right for you, but if you choose carefully—and keep trying until you find the ones that work best in YOUR life—you CAN change!

1) Eat more asparagus, bouillon, lettuce, mushrooms, broccoli, cabbage, celery, carrots, pickles, cauliflower, radishes, spinach, egg whites (not yolks), zucchini, turnips — all low calorie foods.

2) Eat slowly, so you can savor every bite. Make eating a real luxury, fully enjoying the taste of everything. You'll get more fun — and less weight — out of eating! By slowing down, and paying attention to your *food* while you eat, you may find you have less of a "need" to eat, and you'll be less likely to eat when you're not really hungry.

3) This method — and the next several following — works with eating as well as with some of the other habits you may be trying to change: Make an agreement with yourself to eat/smoke/drink *only* in a specified place. Thus, you may choose to eat only at the kitchen table, or smoke only in a particular chair. This is a help in two ways: first, you'll accustom yourself to eating/ smoking/drinking in a chosen place and eventually *not so many places and things will remind you of food/smoke/drink* and lead you to want that; second, you'll likely find it too much bother to go to your chosen place all the time to eat/smoke/drink, so you'll DO that habit less (if you are true to your "contract" with yourself).

4) How about making a few changes in your environment? If you normally pass a food store, bar, or other cue which usually reminds you of the habit, while on your way to or from work, try changing your route. That's easy isn't it? Why keep tempting yourself? And, at home, you can simply not keep extra food/cigarettes/ alcohol/pills in the house. That way, when you want some, you'll have to take the trouble to go out to get it. If it's not available, you'll use it less!

5) Here's another one: Simply record (in a diary of sorts) *when* you eat/smoke/drink/take pills, *how long*

you eat/smoke/drink/..., *how much* you eat/smoke/...,
where you eat/..., and *what mood you're in* as you do
so. I know it's a bother to write it all down, but this
self-monitoring *in itself* will help you to change! Hard
to believe, isn't it? It's true—research has shown that
just keeping track of a behavior can help you to change
it. The other advantage of this approach is that you may
learn some interesting things about your eating/
smoking/drinking/pill taking patterns which can help
in other ways. For instance, do you eat/smoke/drink/
take pills when you're anxious, or under stress, or
alone, or depressed? What "cues" in your environment
seem to trigger your desire for the habit?
Recording has another important benefit: YOU are in
control of the changes you make. Not a doctor. Not a
therapist or group. YOU have the power!

6) Try the "delay" technique: When you get a craving
for food/smoke/drink, tell yourself you can have it
later—in an hour, or later this evening, or tomorrow, or
whenever. Then when that time comes you can have it
(if you still want it). By delaying things you're not
depriving yourself—after all, you can still have the
craved item later on. But often you won't *want* it later
on. And even if you do, the delaying technique has
shown you have the power over your behavior!

7) Change your attitude about not eating/smoking/
drinking/taking pills. (Remember Part One?) For
example, when you find yourself hungry, you needn't
get depressed about it. Rather than thinking, "Am I
hungry! I just can't get through these eating changes,"
say this to yourself instead, "Am I hungry! That's *great*
because it means my body is really attacking those fat
cells!"

8) Substitute: Low calorie foods for high calorie ones.
Activities for smoking. Meditation for drinking. A party
with friends for pills alone. Plan more activities so the
situation doesn't tempt you. Eat lower fat foods (less

meat, lower grade meats, fewer fried foods, margarine instead of butter). Chew gum instead of smoking. Drink cola instead of alcohol.

9) Find out what works for others. There are hundreds of approaches to habit change, diets, stop-smoking plans. In order to really work, a plan must be tailored to YOU. By exploring many different ways, you'll likely hit on the right combination. Ask your doctor, too, but don't *blindly* follow anyone's plan for you!

10) Practice "stress inoculation," so you'll be ready for those inevitable times when you'll be highly tempted to give in to the old habits. "Stress inoculation" works like this:

Make a list of the situations that you consider "high-risk." Then think up some statements you can say to yourself that will help you cope with those situations when they occur. For example, suppose you find it difficult to keep from drinking when you're at a party where alcohol is served or when you've just had a particularly gruelling day. Here are statements that might help you cope: "Boy, many others are drinking (or What a day I've had), and it sure is tempting to have a few martinis. Well, it's natural to feel this way, because this is a high-risk situation for me. Calm down now. That's better. I knew in advance that there would be situations like this. That's OK. I can handle it..."

Got the idea? Make up your own self-statements—decide what would be helpful to *you*—and then imagine the situation (or role-play it with a friend) and say those statements out loud. Do this a number of times (get some good practice in), and then do the same thing again, except now say those statements only in your thoughts instead of out loud.

Use this process for all the types of situations that are likely to be difficult for you. Then, when the situations come up (and they undoubtedly will, from time to time), simply repeat those rehearsed statements to yourself. Studies have shown that "inoculating" oneself before hand to these typical stress situations is very effective in helping people cope when the actual situations occur. (More on this at the end of this chapter.)

It is possible that you may still give in some time and eat/smoke/drink or take whatever other drug you've gotten addicted to. If that happens, it is not the end of the world. Unfortunately, some people let themselves fall to pieces when they break their abstinence. "Oh no. I've failed! Oh well, I might as well keep on *now*—I've already fallen down, and it's too *late* to get back up."

You can use stress inoculation for these times too. Here is an example of self-statements you might rehearse for use in such a relapse situation: "Well, I had a drink (pill, ...). Is that the end of the world? No! Can I regain my control at this point? Certainly! A slip-up here doesn't make me a bad person. It just means I had a situation that was more difficult than my coping skills handled at that moment. That's OK. I'll improve my skills. And I can handle this situation now from this point on."

Remember, practice makes it easier. And it gives you confidence. Or, to be more precise, it shows you that you have the power to handle things. You even have the power to handle the situations where you haven't fully used your power! That's real strength, believe me.

And you've got it!

Exercise. It helps you live longer. And it makes every present day a little more enjoyable. The trick is to do as much exercise as *you* want. Moderate exercise is fine—you don't have to be an athlete or a gymnast to be healthy. For example, I once tried jogging a mile every day. I gave it up eventually because I found that I really disliked it. And I didn't figure the rewards were worth the pain and hassle I put myself through. Unfortunately, a lot of people give up exercising because they think it has to be painful or time-consuming. It doesn't. Pick exercises that appeal to you and that you know you'll take the time to do. Doing a few exercises each day is infinitely better than *deciding* to do a whole lot—and then not following through. Ultimately, what exercises you *plan* on doing won't help your body one bit. It's what exercises you actually *do* that will help you feel more alive.

Just what are the benefits of regular exercising? It helps prevent heart attacks and lung disease, for one thing. It gives you a level of fitness that makes it easier to get things done and makes you comparable to people younger than you. And for many people it makes sleeping easier and gets rid of (or reduces) other health problems (ulcers, fatigue, etc.). In general, exercise helps you feel more ready to face the world, deal with stress, and handle potentially high-emotion arousal situations. It helps you feel good.

I've talked throughout this book about changing the way you look at reality. Rope skipping is a particularly good example of how you can do this. Remember when you were younger and you skipped rope *for fun?* No one told you you *had* to do it for your health (like eating spinach)—you just did it because you liked it. The difference between that and doing it out of duty because you (groan) need the exercise—is your perception. Yes, it's in you. As all of this is.

Walking is a fantastic physical fitness program. It gets just about all of you in shape—and it too is fun. Probably the only way you're going to get this one in, though, is to plan it. So don't take your car to places that are close by. You'll not only save gas money and avoid the hassle of parking—but you'll be giving yourself a real treat and making yourself more physically fit besides. For places that you "have to" drive to, don't park too near your destination. Let yourself enjoy a stroll. I know, that means leaving a little earlier. But it's *nice* to not always be in such a rush. Making a little extra time for a leisurely stroll is also insurance against bad traffic conditions—you see, leaving early is good all around.

For more of a work-out, try swimming, bicycling, or disco dancing. Or try running or jogging a little each day. (If, like me, you don't find jogging all that thrilling, try the "walk-run." That is, run half a block, walk half a block, run again, etc. Or else walk as fast as you can—almost running, but not quite.)

Among many exercises I've found useful: For the back, lie down and put your knees to your chest, or stand up and lean down to touch your toes; for the neck, rotate your head in front of you or turn it back and forth to the sides; for the shoulders, pretend to swim, or reach for the ceiling; for the knees, lie on your back and pedal your feet as if on a bicycle; for the hips, lift up each leg straight up to the side as far as it will go; for the stomach, sit on the floor and lean back gradually without using your arms for support.*

You don't have to do all of these. Do whatever feels realistic for *you*—*and* whatever seems enjoyable to you. You're not in a race against your neighbors, you know, so it doesn't matter whether you're better, faster, or stronger than they are. What matters is that you're making yourself feel better and enjoying playing that game.

In the last analysis, that's what exercising should be about!

Stress. We all have some in our lives. If we didn't, life would be pretty boring. (Can you imagine going through life with nothing to get you excited, nothing challenging to handle?) But often we don't deal with it constructively or we let ourselves be overwhelmed by it, and we cause ourselves both psychological *and* physical problems as a result. Sometimes we deal so poorly with stress and are so unaware of it that we find ourselves anxious, depressed, or with a headache—without even knowing why!

Do you get frequent or severe headaches? Do you have high blood pressure? Do you get tired easily? Do you have skin problems (excessive dandruff, itchiness, inflammation)? Do you get a lot of colds every year? Are you nervous a good deal of the time? Do you get frequent diarrhea, constipation, stomach aches, other aches and pains, dizziness? Do you

---

*See Linde's *Whole Health Catalogue* and Art Ulene's *Feeling Fine.*

have an ulcer or a delicate, ulcer-prone stomach? Do you have heart problems?

A lot of these physical symptoms are triggered by stress. Even allergies and other health difficulties that seem to be purely biological in nature are related to stressful situations. Now, if you suffer from any of the above, that does not *necessarily* mean that stress is the real culprit—there *are* physical causes for these symptoms too. (You'd be ahead to get a thorough physical exam by your doctor.) But often stress is the real culprit—or at least contributes to the other causes.

We all live with stress in our lives. Even when good things happen to us we often get a stress reaction. Here are a number of things that result in stress for most people. Check the ones that have happened recently (or are happening now) in your life:

__ Death—of spouse, other family member, friend.

__ Divorce or separation—and even marriage!

__ Your job—getting fired, getting hired (!), getting retired, having new responsibilities in the job, changing career, or other job changes.

__ Living changes—kids grow up, *you* grow up, you move to a new home, you get (a) new family member(s), you change your eating patterns.

__ Success—yes, even achievements and good luck usually cause stress.

__ Financial matters—you lose a lot of money, you *gain* a lot of money, you have financial difficulties of one sort or another.

__ Arguments, fights, or trouble in general—with family members, friends, in-laws, people at work (your boss or co-workers).

__ Sexual problems—of all kinds.

__ Vacations, family get-togethers, and other "fun" hassles.

__ Noise—running TV sets, radios, and air conditioners;
barking dogs, other people's yelling and screaming—
all of these can raise your tension level. An
experiment was done to demonstrate the bad effects of
noise, with 1,000 subjects: A person drops his books
as he's moving stuff into his house—but he only does
it when a pedestrian is walking by. If there is no major
noise going on in the background, there's an 80%
chance that the pedestrian will help pick the books up.
But if the power lawnmower is going, only *15%* stop to
help!*

This is just a partial list of things that can be stressful. As
you can see, even positive things are on the list. Obviously,
we should have some stress (a completely *un*eventful life with
no challenges or stress at all is bad for your physical and
emotional health too). But it's best not to have too much of it,
whether it's positive or negative. If you find yourself being
irritable, with headaches, or with one of the other stress-
related symptoms I noted earlier, check to see if some of the
above items (or others) are responsible. One way to do this is
to carry around a notebook. For the next few days write down
every time and situation where you find yourself feeling
"uptight," nervous, anxious, etc. Or, when you find yourself
feeling this way and you don't know what has brought it on,
take a few moments to relax and let images come into your
head—they could be people, things, events, whatever. Write
these down. Then cross check them with your list of high-
stress situations and see if you can figure out what may be
contributing to your present stress symptom(s). Another way
to discover the "cause" of your stress is to relax yourself
through the relaxation exercise and imagine that you are
meeting *you* (see yourself, or your identical twin, walking
toward you, for example)—and ask this other "you" what the
problem is. Very often "you" will tell you just what it is.

---

*See Linde's *Whole Health Catalogue*, p. 64.

There are two advantages to finding out what are the "causes" of your stress or anxiety: 1) If you've been suppressing it, just acknowledging the stress-trigger helps to relieve some of the anxiety. 2) Once you know what the "causes" are, you can eliminate or modify some of them.

If you know what things are likely to trigger your stress, you may want to use some of the following suggestions for easing it.

1) As soon after you experience a stress situation as possible, use the relaxation exercise to get yourself into a calm state and then imagine a soothing scene for yourself—a beautiful garden, a sandy beach by a lazy lake, or some other scene that you normally associate with peacefulness. In other words, take a vacation trip from your anxieties through your mind!

2) Some people find that keeping a diary of the day's events, both good and bad, helps them deal more effectively with their stresses. Since so many of us suppress our feelings of anxiety at things when they actually happen, the diary gives you the opportunity to get back to them and find out your reactions. Just write down all the events that happened during the day. Next to each item write an answer to this question: "How did I feel about that?" Don't think too hard—just let the words come naturally. For the items that have anger, sadness, anxiety, or other similar feeling words by them, make a note to institute a few changes in these areas the next day, if possible.

3) One simple way to reduce stress symptoms is to get rid of some of the things that trigger them! Sounds like common sense, but since many of us don't even heed our own common-sense advice, I'm mentioning it here.

Suppose there's a lot of noise in your environment, and that "bothers" you. Then start closing off as much of it as possible—turn off machines, TVs, radios, close doors and windows, whatever.

Or suppose you always get a headache or some other stress

symptom during the holidays because you have the relatives over to one of those big holiday meals. Maybe it's the people. Maybe it's just the hassle of planning the whole thing. But the *simplest* way to get rid of the holiday stress is *not to have your relatives over!* "Oh, but I have to." No you don't. "But who else would do it?" Who says anyone has to? (You *could* all eat out—Dutch treat.)

If you end up still doing those things which trigger your stress, or keeping those things in your environment that trigger it, at least know that you're choosing that—you're choosing some stress over whatever else is your alternative. Which is OK—we all have our own game to play and I'm certainly not going to try to dictate yours.

4) We've seen that one way to reduce stress is to remove the things that trigger it. Another way is to remove *you* from the situations that trigger it.

"I hate the put-downs and snide remarks at cocktail parties." Then don't go to them.

"My father-in-law really 'makes' me uptight." Then avoid him when possible.

"I 'can't stand' being with a group of people who smoke." Who says you have to be with them?

"Crowded places (buses, subways) 'make' me nervous." Stay away from them.

"I always get so high-strung when I stay up late at night." Go to bed early.

"Scary movies and police shows sometimes 'make' me upset for weeks afterwards. What can I do about this?" Don't watch them!

Got the idea? I know, you'd like more complex, "sophisticated" solutions to your problems. Why not try the easy ones first, and save the complicated ones for the problems that don't have easy solutions?

5) Another way to reduce stress in your life is to re-examine the problems you deal with that trigger it—and see if they are really *your* problems or someone else's!

"I just get so upset because my parents don't get along

with each other and I can't get them to stop the nasty things they say to one another." It's not *your* problem! Your parents own that one. You have enough of your own problems without adding on other people's to worry about.

"My daughter made a bad choice in marriage. I don't see how she and her husband will ever be really happy, and it just kills me." That's *her* problem. Why do *you* persist in killing *yourself* over it?

6) Another way to reduce stress is to re-read Chapters 1 through 5 and see that a good many of your stress triggers would stop being stress triggers if you looked at them differently.

7) Learn to say No when you are asked to do things that will entail more stress than you wish to handle. (Re-read Chapter 9.)

8) Sometimes we let a task or other situation "cause" us stress because we let ourselves be overwhelmed by it—we tackle it head on as a whole entity rather than dealing with it piece by piece.

"Oh no, I don't know how I'll ever lose 20 pounds and bring my weight down to normal." Eliminate the stress of dieting—decide on, say, a pound a week. Don't worry ahead. Just concentrate on that one pound for that one week.

"I've got so many books to read for my courses this semester. How will I ever handle it?" Organize your time. Decide which parts of which books you will read today (or this week) and don't worry about all the rest.

Every job can be divided and subdivided into manageable portions. Do it—and you'll divide up the stress into manageable portions too!

9) Exercise helps to reduce stress. So does proper eating and less salt, sugar, and caffeine. Regular practice of the relaxation exercise (daily "meditation") does the same thing. Try one or more of these for a week and see if it makes a difference.

10) Simplify your life. Enjoy more of life's uncomplicated freebies, like quiet conversations, daydreams, sunsets,

poems, and back massages. You don't have to run around all the time to do every little thing. Pick the important items—and then take the time to do them well. And, while you're at it, enjoy them!

11) Stress inoculation is always a good technique to use for those trigger situations that you can't (or don't want to) avoid. Let's say you often experience "food anxiety" when driving by a fast-food restaurant or store. You get an urge to go in and give in—when you really would rather not stuff yourself with unnecessary or unhealthy foods. Once you know this is a high-risk situation, you can "inoculate" yourself against it by rehearsing self-statements which you can say in your mind when the situation comes up. You just imagine the high-risk situation in your mind and say statements to yourself such as these: "Here I am by this hamburger establishment. It won't do me any good to keep thinking about all the things I could be eating, so I won't. I'm prepared for this—I've practiced for it many times. I'll just calm down and drive past. What a feeling of power that will give me! I can handle it. Yes I can!"

Self-statement to use for taking tests, for job interviews, or for accomplishing other new and difficult tasks, might sound like these: "My first job is to use my reason. Can I handle this situation? Yes. Will I make some mistakes? Probably—but that's OK. Even if I don't 'win' at this, I can still be a winner by doing whatever I'm capable of. That's all anyone can be asked to do. And *I* can handle that for sure!"

The important thing here, of course, is not just having a set of statements to say in your head. It's the *practice* that precedes the actual confrontation with the stressful situation, which helps you use your power. And the more you exercise this power, the stronger your power "muscles" become. That's real health for you!

There you have ten ideas for reducing stress in your life: vacation trips through your mind, keeping a diary of your stresses, removing stress-triggers from your life, removing *you* from stress-trigger situations, refusing to let others' problems be *your* problems, changing the way you look at life's inconveniences (see Part One), learning to say No, dividing up your tasks into manageable portions, good health-keeping in general, simplifying your life, and inoculating yourself against too much stress.

These ideas—along with the suggestions in this chapter for wellness, eating, eliminating harmful addictions, and getting good exercise—will help you tune up your body. And that will help you tune up everything else about you. You are a whole person, after all. And the more you nurture every part of this whole, the more power you will unleash—to be the person you really want to be. And *can* be!

Trust yourself—you've got that power!

Part Three:
HANDLE
YOUR FEELINGS

What I am going to suggest in the chapters that follow are methods for coping constructively with your feelings. I'm not going to tell you to wish them away or pretend they aren't there. But I am going to show you that you do have power over them—only, it's a power that must be cultivated, because severe emotional difficulty has no overnight solution. Still, you can gradually become less a victim of feelings and more in charge of them.

13

Defusing Hostility

In this chapter I have a number of suggestions which should help you to reduce hostility—your own and that of others.* The first thing to do to handle hostility is to *admit* it. Don't pretend that you don't have any. Some people hate conflict so much that they never argue or express anger. Or they have been taught that it's wrong to display emotion and so they react to every ugly situation with cool, unflustered "reason." Only they may do a slow burn later, or be depressed from time to time and not know why, or suffer from ulcers, high blood pressure, headaches, or some other ailment. Some married couples never fight because it seems safer that way. Meanwhile a gradual resentment and distance grows because each gets angry at the other but doesn't feel free to express it. What is even more common is this situation: One person holds back hostility for most of the time, thinking "I mustn't lose my temper"—and then finally explodes over something small, much to the surprise of the other. Often a person's anger toward others is so pushed down and hidden that he or she isn't aware of any at all. Some indications of repressed hostility are sarcasm, gossipping, snide humor, and a cynical attitude towards life—all of which are ways of putting other people down in an indirect, "socially acceptable" way—and of course depres-

---

*Some of the ideas I'll be presenting here can be found in a book by Milton Layden, entitled *Escaping the Hostility Trap*, which you may want to read for more detail.

sion, which is often hostility directed to yourself because you don't feel free to direct it toward others.

You know, sometimes all a person needs is permission to be hostile, in order to see just how much she has bottled up inside. I learned that when I was encouraged at a workshop to express my anger toward a family member. I didn't want to admit that I felt hostile toward this person because we were getting along so well and I felt guilty for feeling any resentment. But it was there all right. I was shocked to see just how intense it was.

So, it's better to accept your anger than to bottle it in with unpleasant side effects. However, if you blow up at everybody, you won't have many friends left. What you need is a method not to repress your hostility, but to defuse it. In case you think that's an impossible task, let me give you a few examples of situations where you automatically and quite naturally defuse your hostility.

Say someone kicks you from behind. You suddenly feel hostile, but what if you then look in back of you to see that the person who kicked you, did so because she tripped over something and collided into you? Suddenly your hostility dissipates somewhat and instead you feel sorry for her.

You're driving along and a car comes up from behind and swerves right into yours. Your first impulse is to be angry and say, "That stupid idiot; why can't he drive more carefully?"—until you learn that he crashed into you through no fault of his own; another car hit him and forced him to hit you.

In his book, *Escaping the Hostility Trap*, Dr. Layden gives a personal example. He was in a hurry one day to get change for a quarter from a vendor so that he could make a telephone call. He held out the quarter and said, "Nickels, please." When the vendor asked, "How many nickels?", the author was just about to snap back, "Well, how many nickels do you think there are in a quarter?"—until he saw that the vendor was blind.

What all these examples have in common is that the person

who originally "makes" you feel hostile, turns out not to be at fault. Once you see that, your hostility subsides.

These examples should give you a clue to handling your hostility in other situations. What you need to see is that in most situations where someone does something mean or hostile to you (thus "making" you hostile), it isn't the other person's fault! Once you see that, it will be easier to defuse your own anger. (Easier, I said. Not a sure thing. I'm not offering any panaceas today.)

In order to see that people aren't usually at fault when they say angry things to you or treat you with disrespect, you have to look at life as a series of 3-car accidents. It is, you know. You look at the person who crashes into you, as it were, with mean words or deeds, and you forget that s/he too is the victim of a crash by someone else, and so on. "But," you say, "s/he didn't have to act so belligerently. *I* wouldn't have acted that way." Right. But the other person has a different life experience than you have and perhaps hasn't learned to cope as effectively. If you had had the same history you *would* have acted the same way.

You see, in nearly every situation where you feel hostility, it's a result of feeling lowered. Someone says something mean, treats you with disrespect—and you feel belittled, put down, lowered. The natural reaction to feeling lowered is to become hostile. You can see this when you look at the difference between the put-down attempts that make you angry, and the ones that don't. If the person who says something mean to you has obvious emotional problems and you know that what she's saying has to be taken with a grain of salt, then you aren't as likely to become hostile. If the person who makes the put-down attempt is a child, you are also less likely to feel angry and resentful. If the person attempting to put you down says something that doesn't threaten you at all—say someone tells you that you're dumb when you know you have an I.Q. of 150 or someone says he can't stand your blue eyes and you happen to like them—then again, you're less likely to lash out in anger. In all these cases you don't react with hostility to the attempted put-downs because you don't actually *feel* put down, or lowered.

It's clear, then, that people usually become hostile when they feel lowered. In fact, hostility is an automatic reaction to feeling lowered. Remember that, the next time someone puts you down and you begin to get angry. People can't really help it when they put you down. They have this automatic reaction: When they feel lowered, they try to raise themselves back up by lowering others. They're like the guy who hits your car in a 3-car accident. He couldn't help it—he was propelled into you.

Now, you may still be resentful toward your parents for the way they treated you. Once you realize that they didn't give you the respect you wanted because *they* probably didn't get the respect *they* felt they needed, then some of your hostility will disappear. Why do you think child abuse runs in families? Parents who abuse their children generally turn out to have been abused children themselves. It's an "automatic" reaction. Your parents, your spouse, your friends, your children—all those people who "make" you so mad—they're victims just like you. In a way, they can't help it. Once you see that people's hostility to you is only a reaction to their feeling inferior and unrespected, then *you* won't feel so hostile. You'll feel the same way you'd feel if someone kicked you from behind but then you found out he couldn't help it—he tripped and fell into you. You'll feel the same way you'd feel if someone yelled at you but then you found out her husband died and she can't get herself together. In other words, once you see that, in a way, people can't help feeling hostile, that it's a conditioned response that arises from their own bad feelings about themselves—then at least some of your hostility will change into sympathy.

When I tell people this, they sometimes object: "When I get mad, I get mad, and I'm not going to feel like analyzing other people's inferior feelings." Fine. It's true enough that much of the time you're going to become hostile without thinking. That's OK. Forgive yourself. After all, if it's not the *other* person's fault that she becomes hostile when she feels belittled, then it's certainly not *your* fault either that you react to put-downs with hostility. Don't punish yourself for not being able to turn hostility into sympathy with ease. God knows, most of us punish ourselves for enough already. Accept your hostility and let yourself experience it. Then at *some* point allow yourself to realize that the other person's hostility comes from low feelings of self esteem. This will have the effect of *gradually* changing your way of reacting to hostility. You may not change overnight; but you will *begin* to change.

Now you know how to reduce some of *your* hostility. But what do you do if you live with someone who doesn't know how to reduce his or hers? Well, since most hostility arises from feelings of low worth, of not being adequately respected, the way to help people reduce their hostility is to shore up their feeling of self-worth. You do that by showing them that you respect them. One way to do this is to compliment them when you feel they've said or done something worthwhile. The second thing to do is to admit you are wrong, when you are, or at least the possibility of your being wrong. Have you ever noticed how long a heated argument can go on when both people feel they'll lose out if they give in? Eventually the issue you began arguing over isn't important anymore—winning at any cost is. I have found myself arguing for a position I didn't even agree with, but debating it strongly nonetheless because I didn't want to *lose*. The issue becomes insignificant; it becomes a battle for respect. Once the other person says, "You're right; I've been dumb for arguing this position"—then you are likely to say, "Well, you're not so dumb. Actually, your argument had some good points." Once one person gives respect and esteem to the other, then the other doesn't feel compelled to belittle the first anymore.

"Gertrude, you've overdrawn the checking account."

"*I've* overdrawn! What do you mean? Last time I wrote a check, there was plenty to cover. *Your* check for those electric golf clubs is the one that bounced, Percival."

"But you should have remembered that I was buying those, Gertrude. Why didn't you think before writing another check, you idiot?"

"*Me*, idiot! Why didn't you tell me you were going to make the payment that day? That was definitely dumb, darling."

"This is typical, Gertrude. You write checks whenever you feel like it, without concern for the family. Buying that battery-powered eyebrow pencil sharpener was certainly shelfish."

"Selfish! And how about you? How much time and money do you spend with your outings? You're a perfectly pampered primadonna, Percival."

This is a domestic arms race. Either Gertrude or Percival could de-escalate at almost any point in the discussion by showing respect to the other. If Gertrude did, it might go like this:

"Gertrude, you've overdrawn the checking account."

"Oh no, did a check bounce? I'm sorry, I didn't know there wouldn't be enough to cover my check. Could you help me figure out a system so both of us can avoid overdrawing?"

Percival might have de-escalated by changing his first line:

"Gertrude, I got a note from the bank that we were overdrawn. Can you help me figure out a way to keep this from happening in the future?"

Or, if he wasn't foresighted enough to defuse before the

argument began, Percival still might have de-escalated after Gertrude's first line:

"Gertrude, you've overdrawn the checking account."
"*I've* overdrawn! What do you mean? Your check for those electric golf clubs is the one that bounced."
"You're right. It *was* mine. Is there something we could do so we both know how much money we have in our account?"

Of course, there are times when you can't defuse another person's hostility by showing respect. A person who feels very put down by you or has had a history of being lowered and made to feel worthless may react by still being hostile. You should also remember that it doesn't do much good to compliment someone or admit you're wrong, when you don't mean it. If you say, "OK, OK, you're right, I'm wrong," and you're not sincere, then the other person is likely to become even more hostile. And there's no point in giving a compliment if you can't think of anything honest to say. But if you really do respect the other person, you will be able to show that in some way, if not in the heat of the argument, then later. You don't have to completely give in, by the way. You could say this, for example: "I'm still mad at you, but I will admit you've got some good points." That may not get rid of the other person's anger, but it will probably reduce it.

If you don't have the presence of mind to help lower the other person's hostility, by the way, don't blame yourself. There's no sense in feeling hostile toward yourself for reacting with an automatic reaction to your own inferior feelings. Just make a note of what happened, in your mind; your reactions may change, as so much of life changes— gradually.

A few more suggestions. You probably have some hostility in you now toward certain people—hostility that you've either been repressing completely or saving for a rainy day when those persons load you with the proverbial last straw. Or else there are certain kinds of situations that particularly raise your hostility level. To deal with this, here's a suggestion drawn from implosive therapy (also called "flooding" therapy): Make a list of all the persons and situations that "make" you angry and resentful. Then make a tape recording describing these in full detail, even exaggerating the intensity. The tape should be an hour long and you should listen to it at least five times. The tape won't be too difficult to make — after all, you daydream and night-dream about the mean things people have done to you, all the time, and even about the mean things they might do or could do. Well, get it all on tape. You may get mad all over again when you think of some particularly aggravating events, but by listening over and over (at least five times with an hour-long tape — studies show that you need this much for it to be effective) — your hostility will subside so that eventually the tape will be boring. Then when you are confronted with similar situations in the future, you will be more likely to respond without hostility. One caution is in order here, though. If your anger is such that an hour of thinking about it will arouse more emotion than you feel you can comfortably handle, then start with a 5-, 10-, or 15-minute tape to handle your hostility in smaller doses, before moving on to the hour-long tape. (For particularly troublesome anger or hostility it may be wise to seek out a professional counselor who can help you safely work through those feelings.)

Another way to reduce hostility is to use the relaxation exercise from Chapter 10 and gradually desensitize yourself to hostility (see the next chapter for the details of this technique).

Finally, since raising your own respect will make you less defensive and hostile when others are hostile to you, I suggest reading Chapter 16 of this book, which is on learning to like yourself.

To summarize what I've said here:

1. It's better to experience your hostility than to suffer the side effects of repressed anger.
2. Your hostility automatically begins to defuse when you see that the other person isn't completely at fault—when you see that the guy who smashed into your car couldn't help it because he himself was the victim of a crash.
3. Hostility is usually an automatic reaction to being lowered. When people become hostile, it's not completely their fault.
4. THEREFORE, you can defuse your hostility by recognizing that the *other* person's hostility toward you is probably not his/her fault—s/he's just part of a 3-car accident.
5. You can help defuse another person's hostility by showing respect through an honest compliment or a sincere admission of being in the wrong. This will take away his/her need to belittle you.
6. You can defuse some of the hostility you already have by making an hour-long tape describing the people and situations that "make" you mad and listen to it until it bores you, or else you can use the gradual desensitization technique of relaxation.
7. You can decrease your potential hostility by simply raising your own self-image.

Now, if you're ready to explore more of your feelings and learn techniques for dealing more effectively with them, then read on.

14

Fear, Depression, and Problem Feelings in General

Feeling afraid or anxious often gets in the way of your happiness or fulfillment, as do certain other feelings like depression (or "rejection") and hostility. There are a number of techniques or methods for defusing their bad effects, which I will briefly explain in this chapter.

Before I do, though, I'd like to give you this caveat: There are some emotions that we *think* we want to get rid of but which we either secretly want to hold on to or else don't care enough about to bother to change. For example, I often jump in fear when someone tries to surprise or scare me. (When I was still in school some of my friends used to wait in dark corners and jump out at me, just to watch my reaction— which generally surpassed their highest hopes.) I actually enjoyed (and still enjoy) being scared. (I enjoy riding roller coasters and other "thrill" rides, and I seek out scary and frightening movies to watch.) I also find that often other people find my reactions funny or interesting. So why give up that fear?

My only point in bringing this up is to remind you to be sure you actually *want* to get rid of some of your emotional "problems" before going through the motions of doing so and then pretending you "tried" and giving up.

All of the methods suggested in this chapter are tested and useful as tools for growth on your own. Nevertheless, be sensitive to your own realistic limits, and seek professional

help if you need it. Trust *yourself* first, though!
Now for some methods of defusing problem feelings:

1. *Gradual* [*"systematic"*] *Desensitization.* As noted in Chapter 10, you can use the relaxation exercise to gradually eliminate some of your problem emotions. Behavior modification therapists are the ones who invented this technique, and it has proven to be effective in reducing fear and anger from situations that normally elicit these. It is believed that fear- and anger-arousing situations are only fear- and anger-arousing because of their past associations with these emotions. The way to get rid of their connection with these problem feelings, then, is to condition in a new response that is incompatible with these feelings—namely, a relaxed or calm response. The conditioning is done very gradually, increasing the dosage a little bit more each time, much as you might increase the dosage of allergy immunization injections until you gradually eliminate the allergic response (that's called "desensitization" too). The theoretical explanation underlying this technique has recently been questioned, but the technique itself has proven rather effective.

Here's how to do it. Suppose you become afraid every time you see a dog (or every time you have to give a speech, or every time your friend/spouse/parent/lover criticizes or yells at you). Or, suppose you become angry whenever someone acts a particular way toward you or you have to do a certain task or whatever. If you want to get rid of this feeling response, then make a list of all the situations which elicit it. Then number them in order of emotional arousal—that is, put a "1" in front of the situation that causes only a little feeling, a "2" in front of the one that causes a little more, and so on up the scale. About 8 or 10 items is fine.

For example, let's say you are deathly afraid of dogs. So maybe you'd give a "1" to the situation of seeing a small dog 200 feet away, and a "10" to the situation of seeing a German Shepherd next to you and barking and snipping at you—and you'd number all the situations in between according to how scared you get in each one.

OK, start with situation no. 1. Get yourself relaxed through the relaxation exercise. Then imagine seeing a small dog in the distance (or whatever your lowest-arousing situation is). Now, on a scale of 0 to 100, where 0 equals absolute calm and 100 equals absolute terror, what are you feeling? Your anxiety level will probably rise somewhat when you imagine the situation, but since you're already in a relaxed state, it will be much less than it would be in the real-life situation. OK, now forget the situation and quickly relax yourself again. Then imagine situation no. 1 again. On your scale of 0 to 100, how high is your fear this time?

Keep doing this until situation no. 1 arouses very little anxiety (say, 10 or under). Now move to no. 2. Repeat the procedure until you have gone through your list.

This technique will take some time. How much depends on the strength of the anger or fear. But plan on at least a week with a one-hour session each day. Remember, the gradual desensitization method works with just about any fear- or anger-arousing situation. The new conditioned response of calmness to the imagined situation has a carry-over effect to the real-life situation. Of course, you can also condition yourself while actually experiencing the real situation (rather than just the imagined situation). This is a more effective way to use this technique but is sometimes very difficult to engineer or arrange.

2. *Watching Others Who Deal Constructively with Feelings.* Recent research indicates that many people can overcome some of their negative emotional responses simply by watching others who serve as models. For example, studies have shown that this technique works more quickly than gradual desensitization on phobias like fear of snakes and other animals. People who were extremely afraid of snakes were asked to watch a trainer behind a window who held snakes and let them crawl around on him. Then they

were invited to do the same whenever they felt comfortable doing so. Many did and overcame their fears very quickly.

Now, fear of snakes may not be *your* most pressing emotional problem right now, but the procedure can be used for everyday situations too. For example, suppose you always get angry when you are in a discussion with someone whose views differ sharply from yours—so much so that you usually avoid such situations at any cost. You can eliminate some of your anger response to these situations by watching others who engage in sharp debates *without* becoming "heated" over them.

The same is true of other negative feelings, like depression. If you normally become depressed whenever you think about your divorce or your loss of a loved one or whenever someone says something unkind about you, etc., you can decrease the frequency of your depression response simply by frequently observing a model who responds to the same kind of situation without depression. (It is also true, of course, that you can take on unhealthy emotional responses by continually watching them in others—which is why children so often pick up their parents' pet peeves and anxieties.)

This method of observing persons whose responses are constructive normally takes some time, because you have to find people whose responses make them appropriate as models, and you may have to engineer situations that will provide you with the right kind of observations. A role-playing situation may be about the closest you can get to seeing constructive modeling.

The "watching" method is actually a rather common-sense type of approach. Children and adults learn many behavior skills by watching others who are proficient in them, so why not learn the skills for dealing with life's situations with less emotional trauma, in the same way?

3. *Using I-Messages.* Since anger, when directed at another person, tends to elicit anger in return, consider

expressing the fear or the hurt behind the anger to the other person rather than just the anger, if you want to improve your relationship. That way the other person isn't as likely to become defensive. For example, saying "I'm so mad at you for what you did" is likely to elicit: "What gives you the right—*I'm* the one who should be angry" (or some other hostile response). But "I feel really hurt and low because of this" or "I'm afraid of what's happening in me" is more likely to elicit: "Well, I'm sorry, I didn't mean to put you down" (or some other, more sensitive response).

Expressing your feelings to others as I-messages ("I feel angry," "I feel sad," "I'm afraid") rather than you-messages ("You make me angry," "You make me sad")—will allow others to not be as defensive, because they are not being blamed for *making* you feel something. I-messages are more honest than you-messages, too, because in truth, no one has the power to make you do or feel anything.

4. *Avoiding Negative-Emotion-Producing Situations.* This is a short-cut way to getting rid of some of your bad feelings: Simply avoid those people and circumstances which tend to elicit them. Of course, if you took this to an extreme, you might end up cutting off vast areas of your life simply to avoid hurt, which would be a high price to pay for emotional equilibrium. But certainly you don't have to *always* subject yourself to people or circumstances that elicit unpleasant feelings—you can just choose not to confront them.

I think of the many people I know who visit their families or in-laws over holiday and vacation times—and *hate* it. (I also think of married couples who live together destroying each other.) "What can I do so I won't get so mad/hurt/upset?" they often ask. The most obvious thing to do is not go to be with the people who arouse these feelings! Who says you *have* to be with them, anyway? You've got a choice there, you know.

5. *Practice.* If there are certain situations that are difficult for you to handle because of the uncomfortable feelings that normally come up in them, you can defuse such feelings by practicing a calm response a number of times before entering the situation. This technique is often used in assertion training for cases in which the person has a situation to deal with but feels too nervous or frightened to deal with it assertively. So she or he practices responding the way she would like to, over and over, and then when the real thing comes up she or he is able to do it with a much reduced anxiety level, and with much improved skills.

Practice works so well with other behavioral skills like playing a musical instrument or learning a new job—why not also with personal behavior and feelings?

6. *"Flooding"*—or *Going Through Your Feelings, Over and Over.* I talked a little about the implosive, or flooding method in the last chapter as one way of defusing hostility. It also often works on fear and depression. The idea is simply to experience the emotion and the situation which elicits it (to "flood" yourself with it) so thoroughly that it eventually gets boring.

The implosive method has frequently been used for specific phobias, or fears. For example, someone who is afraid of heights is told to stay somewhere high, say on a high but safe balcony of a tall building, for a full day. The experience is at first very frightening, but eventually the fear is dissipated and at the end of an appropriate period of time one just doesn't have much anxiety left. People who are afraid of other things, like animals or crowds or wide open spaces, are similarly exposed to them for a long period of time, until the fear is exhausted.

If you have a particular emotional difficulty, say, anger at certain people or in certain situations, or fear of certain behaviors or environments, or depression when someone criticizes you or rejects you—then you may want to try the implosive method. Imagine the situation which evokes the unpleasant feelings and let yourself experience those feelings—over and over until you get bored and you just don't feel anything anymore. To help you imagine, you may want to use a tape recording that you listen to over and over (at least five hours' worth—if less, you may increase the problem emotion rather than defuse it). Or else you can have someone help you recreate the problem situation with role playing. I don't recommend this technique if this much experience of your problem emotion will be too difficult for you to safely handle. In that case either begin with frequent smaller doses (e.g., 10-minute sessions) before moving to the hour-long tape; use a different technique altogether (e.g., gradual desensitization); or else see a counselor who can help you handle your feelings through this or another technique.

A friend of mine discovered the flooding method by accident. When she became very angry with someone, she started writing him a letter telling him just how infuriated she was. She wrote page after page, and in order to get her letter to sound just right she even began copying it over, deleting ineffective sections and adding in parts that expressed her feelings with the proper drama and intensity. When she got the letter to sound exactly the way she wanted, she had spent several hours on it—and by then no longer felt the same and thus didn't send the letter after all.

I once worked with a woman who was feeling a lot of anger toward her husband because of what she considered his unfair and dishonest actions toward her. They both worked out some solutions to their problems, and the woman now wanted to get on with the relationship—but her anger kept getting in the way. It would crop up at unexpected times and undermine some of the progress they were making together. So we taped an hour-long session in which she described every incident that had "made" her angry with her husband. Then, using the tape as a resource, she wrote a paper explaining each incident in detail and all the feelings associated with them. Next, I read the paper back to her on tape and asked her to listen several more times to both the original session and my reading of her paper. When you add up the hours this woman spent talking, listening, reading, and writing about her anger, she "flooded" herself rather extensively and found the tapes rather boring at the end. Although not all of the anger disappeared, it stopped being a serious problem for her.

I sometimes use a variation of this approach for myself. If I'm feeling depressed or angry, I express my feelings on tape to my friends and family. (Some of them live far away and so we exchange cassette tape recordings instead of letters.) By the time I've finished explaining my feelings to half a dozen different people on a half dozen tapes — well, I get pretty bored with the problem feelings myself by then.

7. *Increasing Self-Esteem.* Chapter 16 ("Liking Yourself") contains suggestions for improving your liking of yourself, which will in general decrease some of your negative feelings. You see, if you have a good self-image, then you will not have as much fear of situations and people because you will feel confident about handling them. You also won't get as depressed when people hurt you, because you won't be so dependent on their approval — or when things go badly, because you'll have the confidence and the positive attitudes to deal with whatever life gives you. (As they say, "When life gives you lemons, make lemonade.") And you won't become as angry or hostile at people because you won't have the need to lower others through hostility in order to raise your self-respect — you'll already have plenty of self-esteem and thus won't feel such a need.

In general, then, improving your own image of yourself makes anger, fear, and depression easier to handle and less intrusive.

8. *Meditation.* The relaxation exercise described in Chapter 10, when practiced frequently, usually results in your being less subject to problem emotions. Most people who practice it report a decrease in anxiety, aggression, and

depression.

9. *The Two-Chair Method.* Here's a technique from Gestalt Therapy: Set up two chairs and sit in one of them. The one you're sitting in represents you. The other one represents someone else (living or dead) that you have strong feelings about. (Or it could represent some part of *you* that you have feelings about, or even an object or an event). Talk to the person or thing represented by the other chair and tell him/her/it how you feel. Then move to the other chair and *be* that other person or thing and respond. Carry on a conversation this way. (Be sure to move from chair to chair—this helps you psychologically *feel* and *be* both parties.) Make certain that you express your feelings, and not just intellectualizations, as you go on being you and being the other. If your feelings are particularly strong, then say them loudly and express them over and over, using physical gestures too. (I got in touch with my angry feelings toward a family member with this method, and I hit a bean-bag chair with a tennis racket as I screamed obscenities at the bean bag, which for me was that person.) You see, the other person doesn't have to actually be there in the room with you. The other lives inside of you, if you're carrying around feelings about her/him. So you can be that other person yourself and interact, with the result that you not only let bottled-up feelings out, you also discover the other person's point of view by *being* him/her—*and you may resolve your conflict then and there* because you'll gain new understanding into your relationship. So often we hold on to our negative feelings because we can't get inside other people's head to see how *they* feel. The double-chair technique gets you to do that and thus it becomes easier to let loose your bad feelings.

10. *Intensely Examining Your Feelings.* Another method, which can be used right when your bad feelings first happen, is to concentrate on them intensely. If you do this, they will be more likely to fade away. When you try to ignore your

feelings, they are likely to persist "underground," or below your surface consciousness.

Here's how to use this method. Suppose something has happened which has "made" you feel angry, hurt, frightened, or sad. Ask yourself these questions (and as you answer them, feel and experience the answers): What am I feeling right at this moment? What body sensations am I having? (Tightness? Rumbling? Dried up? Twisted? Shakiness? What kinds of pain?) *Where* am I having these sensations? (In my back? Neck? Stomach?) How big an area are they occupying? (That is, how long; how wide; how deep?) If this hurting space could be filled with a liquid, how much would it hold? (A few cups? A thimble-full?) What color does it feel like?

As you describe your body feelings to yourself, they will probably begin to move around, and so you must ask all these questions all over again. Keep concentrating on what is happening in you—be in contact with its every part—and through your examination of it and non-resistance to it, your negative feeling state will likely begin to dissipate.

If you want to impress your friends, by the way, then the next time someone has a headache, try this same method to get it to dissipate. (It has worked almost every time that I've tried it.) A typical conversation often goes something like this:

> You: Where is your headache located—front, back, right side, left side...?
> Other: Uh, it's sort of on the right.
> Y: Near the skin or farther inside?
> O: Farther inside.
> Y: How long is it?
> O: About five inches.
> Y: How wide?
> O: Oh, about an inch and a half.

Y: And how deep?
O: Maybe two inches.
Y: Is it straight or curved or what?
O: It's straight back.
Y: If you could fill it with water, how much would it take?
O: Oh...maybe half a cup.
Y: Is it a sharp sensation or a vibrating one or what?
O: It's kind of going in and out, a throbbing.
Y: What color does it feel like?
O: A blackish brown—maybe a little green too.
Y: Fine. *Now* where is it located?
O: It's still sort of on the right.
Y: How long is it?
O: About five inches.
Y: How wide?
O: Two inches.
Y: How deep?
O: Well, now it's hardly deep at all—it's sort of flat.
Y: How is it shaped?
O: It's kind of an L-shape now.
Y: How much water could it hold?
O: Oh, just a little...like, one eighth of a cup.
Y: What kind of sensation is it?
O: Well, it's not throbbing now. It's just sort of there... constant.
Y: What color is it?
O: Uh, red, I guess. ...
Y: Good. *Now* where is it located?
O: On the top of my head now, right in the middle.
Y: How long?
O: About seven inches.
Y: And how wide?
O: Gee, only a half inch or so.
Y: And how deep?
O: Uh, it's really pretty flat.
Y: What is its shape?
O: Just straight, I think...

Y: If you could fill it with water, how—
O: Hey, it's gone. I can't find it!...How did you do that?

Actually, you may find this method almost enjoyable. It is sometimes very interesting to feel what is going on in your body and to actually locate it and describe it and experience it moving on to different parts of your body before it finally disappears. Even the pain of it isn't so bad when you have the game of watching where it goes.

11. *Intensely Examining the "Causes" of Your Feelings.* I've talked about examining your feelings and describing them in terms of body sensations. Another way to defuse them is to examine what appear to be their "causes." Suppose, for example, that you are feeling depressed. Then start asking yourself questions like these (and answering them): Why am I depressed? (Because Helen hurt my feelings.) How did she do that to me? (She criticized me.) Why does that bother me? (Because I feel put down.) Am I really put down? (Well, in her eyes I am.) Am I sure about that? (Well, no. But...well, she was right in what she said, so I do feel I am low.) Even if she was right, how am I low? (Well, I'm certainly low in that one area.) So that makes me low in general? (No, I guess not...) Besides, just because she criticized me, and even if she is right—which is open to question—how does that make me low? (Well, I guess I mean I feel depressed.) What is making me depressed? (My bad feelings, or image, about myself.) Why am I imaging this way? (I don't know. I guess I don't really have to.) How am I feeling right now? (I'm sort of mad now, I think.) Why is that? (Because she wasn't very tactful or sensitive.) How does that cause my anger? (Well, I feel like I want to get back at her for putting me down.) Why do I feel that? (Because I just don't have enough confidence in myself to not let things like that bother me.) Why is that? (I guess I just don't like myself that much.) Don't I? (Well, I do, yes, but I don't feel

completely sure of my worthwhileness.) What am I feeling right now? (Uh, not as mad or hurt anymore. Just sort of peeved.) If I could rate my feelings on a scale of 0 to 100, with 0 meaning complete calm and 100 meaning extreme anger, where would I be? (Well, I was about 50 there for a while. I think I'm only 25 right now.) Why am I still feeling this way?...

Just keep asking those questions. Follow the "causes" wherever they take you and you may just explore them right out of you!

12. *Changing Your Thoughts.* Here's a technique from Rational Emotive Therapy (RET), which is similar to the above.* The idea is this: In between everything that supposedly "makes" us feel what we feel, and whatever it is that we feel—are certain thoughts or beliefs we hold. For example, if someone criticizes me and I get depressed over it, it's not the criticism which caused my depression. Nobody's criticism has the *power* to make me depressed. How do I know this? Well, not everybody *else* gets depressed when they're criticized—so the criticism in itself must not have the power to do it. Something else is happening here to help make the connection between criticism and depression. Part of that something is my thoughts, or beliefs, about criticism. If I can change my thoughts on the matter, I will begin to weaken the connection that criticism and depression have for me. I say "begin" to weaken, because just changing your thoughts doesn't accomplish miracles overnight. That's why RET counselors have their clients make a contract to spend some time every day (say, ten minutes) arguing away their irrational thoughts or beliefs about whatever it is that's bothering them. (In this case, it would probably be the irrational belief that criticism of you implies you're not an OK person.) In order to help keep yourself on the right track, you

---

*Rational Emotive Therapy is also sometimes called Rational Behavior Training, and, simply, Rational Therapy.

can reward yourself with something you like for doing your "homework" (disputing your irrational beliefs away) and "punish" yourself if you don't. What do you like—TV, ice cream, a night out? Then give one of these things to yourself each time you fulfill your 10-minute disputation, and make yourself do or have something you *don't* like if you fail to do so.

OK, now let's look at how to actually dispute the irrational beliefs you have which elicit your bad feelings. I'll use a personal example here to help you get the general idea, so that you can dispute with yourself those particular thoughts or beliefs you hold that tend to keep you in an emotional rut.

Let's say you get depressed whenever you hear people say they don't like you or whenever someone criticizes you for something you've done. (This is a problem I've often had.) Then the irrational belief you hold is probably this one: "I'm not worthwhile unless everybody likes me."

Now let's argue against that belief and prove how irrational it is. To begin with, you probably wouldn't be worthwhile if everyone *did* like you—because then you would have to be something like a jellyfish, always changing to be something likeable for everybody. And do you realize that if you were that plastic, or flexible, there wouldn't really be any you? All you would be is a mirror for other people—but nothing in yourself. Besides, once people *realized* that you were such a piece of putty, some of them would *really* dislike you. So, it's clear that you can't please everybody—because if you could, there would be some who'd be displeased by the fact that you could!

OK, now we've got it straight that it is *impossible* to have everybody like you or like everything about you. So your worthwhileness can't depend on that, because if it did, then *nobody* would be worthwhile (since nobody is universally likeable).

Now let's look at the qualities you have which some people don't like about you or which they criticize you for. Are these qualities bad? Well, that's pretty relative. I mean, some people will *like* you for the very qualities that lead others to *dislike* you. (That's certainly true in my case. What some people like in me and call "enthusiasm" and "fun-lovingness"—others dislike and call "immaturity.") Suppose you are extroverted—you like to talk a lot, maybe be the center of attention. Some people will love you for it—they'll enjoy listening to what you have to say, they'll appreciate your clowning, they'll feel more secure and comfortable knowing there's someone like you around who seems to be in control and not afraid to speak out. *Others* will hate you for exactly the same thing—they'll call you egotistical, self-centered, and garrulous. Who is right? Nobody. Because it's all pretty relative. Being extroverted is both likeable and dislikeable. The same is true of every other quality you have. Even if you haven't been criticized for something yet, you can just bet that there are people living in this world who won't like you (or wouldn't like you if they knew you)—for *any* quality you have. Do you do kind things for people? There are people who would hate you for it. ("Boy, what a phoney do-gooder *she* is—look at her doing all those stupid nicey-nice things for people.") Are you creative? There are plenty of people who would hate and envy you for that. The same would be true regarding intelligence or good looks (which are also relative to the eye of the beholder, I might add). There isn't one thing you could do or be that everybody would like.

And, there are probably very few things you could do or be that everybody would *dis*like. Are you shy? Many people are very attracted to shy people. Are you self-centered? Some people are crazy about that—they want people like that around so that *they* can be the giving ones; or else they think of selfishness as independence and they admire it. Do you hate yourself? Some people will love you for that and call you wonderfully humble!

Now that you know you can't depend on other people to decide whether you're worthwhile or not (because they don't all agree—about you or about anybody else), you can see that worthwhileness has nothing to do with a popularity contest.

(If we judged people's worth on popularity contests, then all the so-called great people in history would lose—like Jesus, Socrates, Abraham Lincoln, and every other significant political, religious, or other leader.) Even if your worthwhileness did depend on the vote of other people, it would still make a difference who's doing the voting. Are we to consider your worthwhileness dependent on a 51% majority vote of the world's four billion inhabitants? Or shall we include only some? And what about the people of past or future generations?

No, it's obvious that even a popularity contest wouldn't give you any objective measure of you. So who is going to decide whether you are worthwhile or not? You could let it be decided by the people *you* respect or like. But then some of *them* have obvious blind spots and, at the very least, different taste from yours. I mean, *they're* not perfect, and even if they were, they would still have different likes and dislikes concerning food, art, clothes, entertainment, and yes, personality!

So ultimately, who is competent to decide which of your qulities are good ones and which are bad? You, of course. And even *then*, you can't judge your worthwhileness simply on the basis of those—for several reasons. For one thing, you are a mixture of good and bad (*everyone* is). And you will *never* get to the point where you will be all good or all bad (*no one* does). You will *always* be a combination of good and bad, no matter how much better or worse you get later on. And as long as you have at least *some* good, you'll be worthwhile. Right?

Since all you can do is work at making yourself more good (and *not* become *all* good—ever), then there's no way you or anyone else can get rid of all the bad. So worthwhileness obviously can't be contingent on that.

Besides, don't you realize that *qualities* are not the way to measure anything anyway? You see, qualities are labels we give to people who exhibit certain behaviors. They are not real in themselves. They're just abstract names for things.

For example, when we say someone is a *kind* person, all we mean is that the person has done behaviors that we call kind (and don't forget, not everybody would agree on what is kind and what isn't). But just because a person has done kind things in the past, that doesn't mean he will *always* do them. So the label "kind" is a temporary label. It's an after-the-fact label. It just says where a person has come from, but not where she is at the present (or where she'll be in the future).

So even if you *could* judge a person's worthwhileness on the basis of how much good versus how much bad that person had—it would *still* be impossible to make a judgment because no one is static enough to be labelled that way. Every person is an ongoing process, changing from moment to moment. Human beings don't stand still, so any labels we put on them are obsolete as soon as we attach them. (Besides, even if that weren't true, how would you *ever* decide how much good it takes to overshadow the bad? Good and bad are not like cooking ingredients that can be measured as 51% sugar and 49% salt. Good and bad are abstract words we use that have no absolute standard to be measured against—even if we *could* get people to agree on what's good or bad in every situation.)

If people don't like you or if they criticize you (and if you haven't found those people yet, don't worry, you will—or at least you *would* if enough people found out about you)—then why not think of them as being of a different religion or political persuasion from you? Now, the way you *live* represents what you really believe, so if people don't like the way you live and act, then they're really not liking you for your beliefs either. Think of your life as your own religious or ideological message. Some people will like it and some won't. Not everybody likes the same religion or political message or other ideology. Different people believe different beliefs. Live *your* beliefs and let those who are attracted to them come your way, and those who aren't not. You can even see yourself as a kind of prophet (each of us is, in a sense) with some people hearing your message and others turning away.

You wouldn't be a true prophet if no one was ever offended by you. So carry on the good news as you see it!

That's probably enough "disputation" to show you how to argue against the irrational beliefs you hold which tend to cement certain situations with problem feelings. You can do the same with fear, anger, or whatever else you have difficulty with. Chapter 13, for example, showed you how to change your thoughts or beliefs regarding hostility (by seeing that the person who "makes" you hostile is usually really the result of a 3-car collision). Here is a list of irrational beliefs that RET therapists have developed, which you may want to analyze to see if they are ones that keep you in your rut:

1. I have to be loved and approved.
2. I have to be completely competent, or I'm no good.
3. People that I think are bad deserve to be punished.
4. It's awful when things don't go the way I want them to.
5. I can't create my own happiness—I have to depend on outside people and events.
6. People should take care of me—they owe me that.
7. I'm a victim of my past, and I can never be any different.
8. I just can't stand some people's behavior—I can't *live* with it!
9. Life should be fair.
10. There's a perfect solution to every problem, and it's awful when you don't find it.

Crazy beliefs, aren't they? And yet so many of us operate with these as our hidden assumptions—and thus give ourselves more emotional upsets than we need to have. I won't say that changing your irrational thoughts or beliefs will break all your conditioned anger, fear, or depression responses overnight. But it will help. Especially with time.

There you have it. A dozen techniques for making it easier to handle problem feelings. Some of them are meant to use primarily *when the feelings arise*: (3) using I-messages; (10) examining your feelings; and (11) examining the "causes" of your feelings. Some are designed for use not in the actual situation but in preparation for it: (1) gradual desensitization, (2) watching models, (4) avoiding negative - emotion - producing situations, (5) practice, and (8) daily meditation. And then some can be used either in the situation (or right after) or in preparation for such situations in general: (6) the implosive method, or going through your feelings over and over till they're boring, (7) increasing self-esteem, (9) the Gestalt method, or two-chair technique, and (12) the RET method of changing, or disputing, your irrational thoughts or beliefs.

Use whichever techniques you think are the most reasonable and do-able ones. Experiment a little. And get special help if you need it.

And remember, if you end up not using any of these or any other methods you've heard about, then that means only one thing: You apparently prefer to *keep* your problem feelings rather than to bother defusing them.

And that's OK too.

15

Overcoming Guilt Feelings

Guilt is really a kind of depression (often connected with anger and/or anxiety) resulting from some behavior or feeling of yours which you have been taught is wrong. The methods noted in Chapter 14 are generally applicable to this problem feeling—but since guilt is so pervasive today as a special problem, and since it is usually connected with behavior and values clarification, I have devoted a separate chapter to the subject.

Let's begin our analysis of guilt, then, by clarifying its "causes."

Every time you feel guilty, it's because you have gone against some principle; you've broken some standard. The way to know whether your guilt feelings can be productive or not is to see whether the standard you've broken is one that *you* believe in or not. That is the one simple rule, though it's often hard to apply. If the principle you've gone against is one that you have thought about and reasoned about and accept as your own, then your resultant guilt feelings can be helpful because they will remind you that you haven't lived up to what you want to be, and you can make some changes. But if the standard you've broken is a standard given by your parents or some other authority, which you haven't reasoned out and accepted as your own, then the guilt is not constructive and you need to learn not only how to cope with it but how to get rid of it and keep it from cropping up again.

Let's look at a few examples of unproductive guilt feelings. Someone wants you to contribute your time to a cause, and you're all contributed out, but you feel guilty for saying no. The standard you have broken is the one that says, "You must always help people, no matter how hard it is and no matter how much you hate to." That's a rule you picked up somewhere along the line—perhaps from your parents, your school, your church—and it's not really a very good rule. Because, unless you're hyperactive and a little bit crazy, you're not going to be *able* to always give of yourself. Or if you find yourself feeling guilty for being attracted to people other than your spouse or boy/girlfriend, remember that the standard you have broken is the one that says, "Once you're married (or going with someone) you should never look at another man or woman because true love means being an island of two." Probably not a sensible rule.

One more example. You have probably heard people tell you about the hunger in the world and about how you should contribute your money to agencies that help the poor. And you will undoubtedly hear it talked about in the future. Some people in my congregation have told me that when they hear me talk about injustices in the world or in the community, they feel guilty, especially if they're not doing much about them. If *you* feel guilty, remember that your guilt feelings arise from a standard you've broken, in this case the standard that says, "You should care about what happens in the world and you should personally do something to help the poor." Look at that standard and decide whether it is *your* standard or someone else's. Maybe your parents always told you to eat everything on your plate because there were people starving in India, and so now you feel guilty when you are reminded of how much you have and how little the poor have. Well, if you *don't* agree with the principle that you're supposed to be so concerned about the world, then there's no point in feeling guilty every time the subject is brought up. Those guilt feelings are not constructive because they don't lead to change—they just make you continually feel bad. Now, if you do agree with the principle of caring about social causes, and you're feeling guilty because you're not giving anything or doing anything, then *start* doing something. Because if you really believe you should show concern, and yet you don't, there will be bad effects on your psyche. You see, when you feel guilty for breaking a standard that you don't believe in anymore, at least you can shrug your shoulders and say, "Gee, that's nothing to get upset over." But when you feel guilty for breaking a standard you've accepted as your own and you *still* don't do anything to change, then you will eventually downgrade yourself; you'll put yourself down as a selfish, bad person; and you'll begin to dislike yourself. And that's not a good way to be. So either do something to change your life or else change your moral beliefs, so that you don't have to feel guilty all the time.

The way to decide whether guilt feelings are productive or not seems simple enough: Just look at the standard or principle that you broke which gave rise to the feelings. If it's a standard that you rationally accept as your own, then your guilt feelings are healthy, and you should be grateful that you have an emotional warning system to tip you off that you're not being what you want to be—so that you can change. If it's a standard that is someone else's, and not your own, then the guilt feelings are unproductive. This rule of thumb seems pretty simple, but of course in life it's sometimes difficult to decide just what moral standards we should accept as our own and which ones we should discard. Is it OK to have sex with someone other than your spouse or girl/boyfriend? Is it OK to get high on pot or booze? How high? And how about driving home afterwards? Is it OK to yell at people when you're mad because that makes you feel better, even though it may hurt someone's feelings? Is it OK to say no when somebody really needs your help but you feel you need time for yourself?

And then there are the questions of degree. Yes, I should be concerned about social justice, but how concerned? Should I give most of my money to the poor and live like a hermit, or should I write out a check for twenty bucks to a good cause once in a while, or should I do something in between? Yes, I should be politically involved, but how involved? Is it enough to speak up once in a while or vote at election time, or should I get actively involved in some political campaign? Yes, I have obligations to my family, but how much time do I deserve for myself to be out with friends or to pursue my own career and interests? Yes, I should keep a balance between doing for myself and doing for others, but just where do I draw the line? And where do I draw the line between all the ideals I would like to live up to and the realities that I'm capable of at this point in my life?

What I'm suggesting here is that you should get very *specific* about your ethical obligations. None of this "I will simply love my neighbor" business—that is so general, you'll never know if you've accomplished it or not. Rather, ask: What is my *specific* responsibility in this particular situation? For example, when my spouse or other family member suggests that I stay home and spend some time with the family instead of doing a hobby or attending a meeting or having fun with my friends, then I've got to translate my general values into specific responsibilities. I can't be content with a general platitude like, "A good wife or husband (or son/daughter) spends time with the family." That doesn't give you any real direction. All it does is help you feel guilty anytime you do something just for you. Get specific. "My obligation, my responsibility as a parent/spouse/child/ sibling is to spend 'x' amount of time with my family per week/day."

I know of a man whose mother constantly telephoned, asking him to come over to visit and help with household chores. He resented this infringement on his lifestyle, but he had always been taught to honor his parents, and he never seemed to be able to do enough. (Actually, he would probably *never* be able to do enough for his guilt-inducing and manipulative parents, even if he spent every minute with them!) However, once he was able to abandon general platitudes like, "A good son is always there to help his parents," and once he was able to decide just how far his responsibility lay, *then* he was able to work out a way to both do his own thing and satisfy his obligation to spend time with his mother. He decided that five hours a week was a reasonable visit, told his mother he'd be there on Sundays for that amount of time and would help with anything that needed to be done during that period, and he didn't feel guilty anymore when his mother called to complain about his not being home. Because now he was satisfied with his behavior. You see, when your values are expressed only as glittering generalities, then you can never fulfill them. You can never do enough, so you always feel guilty. But when you specify the contours and limits of your responsibility, then you can do something about them.

Here's a personal example of how I developed a way to deal with my standards. When I first began to learn about injustices in the world, like hunger and poverty, I felt I had an obligation to do something to lessen them. But I didn't know how much I should really do, so I did nothing, and then I felt guilty almost all the time. Then I clarified for myself just what my obligation was and I decided to give a certain percent of my income to causes that I believe foster social justice. And what was left over, after taxes and other basic expenses, I decided to spend mostly on myself. And now, even though I'm concerned about world hunger, I never feel guilty about eating a good meal or just generally spending money on myself, because I'm following the standards that I set for myself. I may decide to do more in the future (or less)—but I feel comfortable with what I'm doing now.

Most of us never bother to just sit down and decide exactly what we think about so-called moral matters. In fact, we may feel it's crass or not "nice" to decide how many hours to give to parents, family, or others—somehow setting limits and reducing things to numbers makes us seem like computers. But the alternative is to never know whether you're doing what's right, and thus feel guilty much of the time. Some of the people who indignantly say, "How can you reduce your love for your parents to five hours a week," are the very same people who don't even give that much (or else they give more but feel—and show—resentment). Getting specific doesn't just mean *reducing* what you give—it often means increasing it. And don't worry—you can always change your amounts and percentages later on as your standards change (and they probably will).

The first step, then, in dealing with guilt, is to set up our own moral standards with specific amounts as guidelines, so we'll know whether we're accomplishing them or not. Some of these standards may be nearly the same as the ones that our parents or teachers or peers told us when we were children, but if they are, the difference will be that we accept them now because we have reasoned them out and not because someone else foisted them upon us. After you have written out some of your own rules of morality, share them with your friends and maybe add some, subtract some, or modify what you have, after you've heard other people's ideas. You know, I've known people who suffered great guilt because they set impossible moral standards for themselves, thinking that everyone else had the same high standards. Just finding out that not everyone else is that "pure," or even wants to be, can be a relief. And then there are some people who set low standards for themselves, even though they are dissatisfied with their superficiality, because they never talked to someone who had higher ideals. Even though only you have the right (and power) to decide your own personal rules, still, sharing your values with others can help you avoid both of the above problems.

I know how tough it is to deal with the questions of values and moral standards. Sometimes we want them to be handed us from some source of authority, such as the church, or the government. Or we may prefer not to think about them at all, and to deal with each situation as it comes up. While those two extremes do work for many people, learning to trust yourself means facing the tough questions on your own terms, and coming up with answers which are right for *you*.

To help you get more specific about some of these issues, I've put together a series of questions on each of thirteen moral/ethical topics. As you read them, don't be limited by the choices I've listed. Simply let this material help you to *think about* the issues involved. Don't use this as a "multiple choice" check list. Then you'd just be choosing one of *my* answers. Instead, write in your own position on the issue, in your own words, on the line provided. If you don't have a firm idea yet, that's OK, but that will be an area you'll want to give some thought. Remember too, that your values, and mine, will change with time and experiences. Allow yourself some flexibility!

HONESTY

- ☐ It is never OK to lie.
- ☐ It is OK to lie, but only if great harm to others will result otherwise. (specify what kind of situation)
- ☐ It is OK to lie, but only if some harm to others might result otherwise. (specify)
- ☐ It is OK to lie if great harm to myself will result otherwise. (specify)
- ☐ It is OK to lie if some harm to myself will result otherwise. (specify)
- ☐ It is OK to tell "white lies" if it's possible someone's feelings might be hurt otherwise.
- ☐ It is OK to tell "white lies" to protect myself or my image.
- ☐ It is OK to lie just about anytime.
- ☐ _____

Comment:

TIME FOR OTHERS

☐   I feel that I owe _____ hours a

    ☐ day
    ☐ week   ☐ be with
    ☐ month   **to** ☐ help
    ☐ year   ☐ (other)

    ☐ my mother
    ☐ my father
    ☐ my spouse
    ☐ my lover
    ☐ my children
    ☐ my siblings
    ☐ my family
    ☐ (other).

☐   I don't feel I owe anyone my time.
☐   _____

Comment:

VIOLENCE—PHYSICAL

☐   It is never OK to physically hurt anyone.
☐   It is OK to physically hurt someone, but only in self defense.
☐   It is OK to physically hurt someone, but only in self-defense or if the other person agrees (e.g., an agreed-upon fight).
☐   It is OK to physically hurt someone if that person has verbally abused me.
☐   It is generally OK to physically hurt someone.
    (Specify below if your position applies to particular persons only.)
☐   _____

Comment:

VIOLENCE — NON-PHYSICAL

- ☐ It is never OK to hurt anyone in any way.
- ☐ It is OK to say or do something that will hurt someone, but only if it will also help that person more.
- ☐ It is OK to say something that may hurt someone, but only if that person has hurt me.
- ☐ It is OK to say something that may hurt someone, but only if I am really angry.
- ☐ It is OK to say OR *do* something that may hurt someone, but only if that person has hurt me.
- ☐ It is OK to say or do something that may hurt someone, but only if I am really angry.
- ☐ It is OK to say or do something that may hurt someone if I'm feeling upset.
- ☐ It is OK to say or do something that may hurt someone whenever I feel like it.
  (Again, if some of these apply to particular persons only, specify below.)
- ☐ _____

Comment:

OBEDIENCE TO LAWS

- ☐ It is never OK to break the law.
- ☐ It is only OK to break the law under extreme circumstances (e.g., self survival).
- ☐ It is only OK to break the law if a higher moral value takes precedence.
- ☐ It is OK to break "unimportant" laws (speed limits, parking regulations).
- ☐ It is OK to break the law if "most everybody does it."
- ☐ It is OK to break the law if I am not likely to get caught.
- ☐ It is OK to break the law occasionally.
- ☐ It is OK to break the law whenever I feel like it.

☐ _____

Comment:

FRIENDSHIP

☐ I should always take the initiative in making friends.
☐ It is extremely important to work at making and maintaining many friendships.
☐ It is valuable to make and be loyal to a few close friends.
☐ It is important to have as many acquaintances/casual friends as possible.
☐ One's need for friends depends upon circumstances: age, family, job,...
☐ One should be friendly to everyone, and not be concerned about "close" friends.
☐ One should be self-sufficient, and not need friends.
☐ I couldn't get along without my close friends.
☐ I don't need anyone but myself.
☐ I should always wait for other people to invite me to be a friend.

☐ _____

Comment:

ACTING RESPONSIBLY

☐ It is always necessary to act in a totally responsible manner.
☐ It is important to be as responsible as one can manage.
☐ "Responsibility" varies with time and circumstances. Just do your best.
☐ Everyone should be held accountable for his/her

behavior.
- [ ] "Responsibility" is a middle-class-Anglo hang-up. Relax!
- [ ] It is important to act irresponsibly once in a while.
- [ ] I'm not responsible to or for anyone. If it feels good, I do it.
- [ ] It is important to always do what I agree to do.
- [ ] It is important to always do what is expected of me.
- [ ] It is OK to "kick back" once in a while, even if I don't get my job done.
- [ ] If someone else is depending upon me, I must always come through.
- [ ] _____

Comment:

COURAGE

- [ ] I ought to be able to be strong and cool under all circumstances.
- [ ] It is OK to let down once in a while, but "big boys don't cry."
- [ ] I need to be careful that no one else sees me as "weak."
- [ ] I can be brave in most situations, but sometimes it's OK to be scared.
- [ ] "Courage" is a cultural hang-up; no one is really brave.
- [ ] It's OK to be scared sometimes. Most people are.
- [ ] It's normal to be scared most of the time in our crazy world.
- [ ] _____

Comment:

SEX—BEFORE MARRIAGE

- ☐ Sex before marriage is never OK.
- ☐ Sex before marriage if OK, but only with someone I'm engaged to marry.
- ☐ Sex before marriage is OK, but only with someone I deeply love.
- ☐ Sex before marriage is OK, as long as it is with someone I know at least casually.
- ☐ Sex before marriage is OK, even with a stranger.
- ☐ _____

Comment:

SEX—AFTER MARRIAGE

- ☐ It is never OK to have sex with someone other than my spouse.
- ☐ It is OK to have sex with someone other than my spouse, but only if both my spouse and I have agreed on this.
- ☐ It is OK to have sex with someone other than my spouse, but only if there is virtually no chance that my spouse could be hurt.
- ☐ It is OK to have sex with someone other than my spouse, regardless of agreement or consequences in general. (Also, specify the limits of sexual activity, if any, in these areas, as applicable—e.g., kissing, petting, etc.)
- ☐ _____

Comment:

ALCOHOL AND OTHER DRUGS

- ☐ It is never OK to get high.

☐ It is OK to get a little high once in a while. (Specify: Once a month? Once a week? etc.)
☐ It is OK to get a little high whenever I feel like it.
☐ It is OK to get drunk/stoned once in a while. (Again, specify.)
☐ It is OK to get drunk/stoned whenever I want to.
☐ _____

Comment:

CONTRIBUTIONS TO HUMANKIND

☐ I should give money/time to just about any individual or organization that asks for my help. (If so, how much? $___)
☐ I should contribute ___% of my income (or $___ per year) to humanitarian causes, specifically, for

        ☐ world hunger
        ☐ local hunger
        ☐ civil liberties
        ☐ religious organization(s)
        ☐ ecology
        ☐ peace
        ☐ political causes
        ☐ _____(others: specify)
        ☐ _____

                      ☐ day
☐ I should contribute___hours per ☐ week to a human-
                      ☐ month
                      ☐ year
itarian cause. (Specify.)

☐ _____

Comment:

WHEN IS IT STEALING?

If by mistake I receive more money than I should (a sales clerk accidentally gives me extra change, a company forgets to bill me for the total amount I owe, the I.R.S. sends more return than I'm entitled to, etc.), it is   □ OK   □ not OK to keep it.

If I receive a service, product, or money because the giving party (e.g., a company) has made a mistake about my age, place of residence, or some other item which would qualify me to receive it, then   □ it is my duty   □ it is not my duty to inform the giving party so that I no longer receive the benefit.

It is □ OK   □ not OK to use every legal loophole I can to reduce my income taxes.

It is □ OK   □ not OK to lie about my age, my place of residence, or some other item in order to get something at a lower cost, or no cost at all, so long as it won't cost the other party (company, organization) any extra money.

It is □ OK   □ not OK to lie about my age, my place of residence, my ethnic background, in order to get something at a lower cost or no cost, period.

It is □ OK   □ not OK to "fudge" my income tax returns a little. (Specify how many dollars it is OK to fudge on, or what percent of my income: $_____, or _____ %.)

It is   □ OK   □ not OK to fudge my income tax returns. (Specify how much: $_____)

Comment:

It is OK to shoplift

☐ never
☐ as long as I take a small item. (Specify cost: $____)
☐ as long as it's from a large corporation.
☐ as long as I do it only infrequently.
☐ regardless of size of item.
☐ regardless of size of store/company/corporation.
☐ as often as I want.
(Check all that apply.)

It is OK to take something that isn't mine

☐ never
☐ in a life-or death situation.
☐ in another emergency (_____).
☐ when I need it very much.
☐ when I feel I deserve it more than the party I'm taking it from.
☐ when I feel I deserve it, period.
☐ when I really want it.
☐ as long as it's not worth more than $____.
☐ as long as I won't get caught.
☐ whenever I feel like it.
(Check all that apply.)

☐ All kinds of stealing are OK.
☐ Just about all kinds of stealing are OK.
☐ Some kinds of stealing are OK.
☐ Just about no kind of stealing is OK.
☐ No kind of stealing is ever OK.
☐ _____

Comment:

Once you have worked out a rough value system for yourself, the next step in dealing with guilt is this: when you're feeling guilty, check out which standard you've broken. If it is truly your own, then apologize for the wrong, make up for it if you can, and resolve to do better next time. But don't give away your last piece of candy or volunteer for every project under the sun or do something else which isn't really a part of your standards, just to get rid of guilt feelings. If you're going to do something nice, do it because it's reasonable for you and a part of your moral standards. Otherwise, you'll end up being resentful.

If you find yourself feeling guilty over something that *isn't* against your standards, then take steps to defuse it. Talk about your guilt feelings, to yourself and to others, and accept them as natural carry-overs from childhood experiences. Throughout all the years of your growing up—from birth until now—you've been rewarded for doing this and punished or scolded for doing that. And so, because of that conditioning, you will often feel anxiety or guilt for things that you were told not to do in your past—even though you no longer feel they're bad. That's natural. So don't try to repress your feelings by saying, "Boy, this is a dumb thing to feel, and am I dumb for feeling it." Sure, it's dumb to feel guilty or scared or nervous over petty things, but we all do and it's quite natural. Instead of repressing your guilt feelings, talk about them. And don't let other people tell you it's dumb to feel the way you do, either. If they do, tell them, "Yes, I know it's dumb, but I feel guilty anyway." Just accepting your guilty feelings and having someone else hear you and understand you will help you overcome them. And then, of course, there are the methods of overcoming problem feelings in general, to be found in Chapter 14, which can also be used for particularly nagging guilt.

Here's a small personal example. One day I was parked in a parking lot that had a sign saying "No Parking." And when I went in to drive out, the proprietor called out, "Buddy, you're not supposed to park here," and he proceeded to bawl me out. As I left I felt very guilty. I felt just like I felt when a clergyperson or parent or some other moral authority figure scolded me as a child, even though I hadn't really done anything that I thought was that bad. Now, I could have just thought, "I shouldn't feel this way," and simply tried to forget the feeling. But then it would have gnawed away at me. So instead, I said to myself, "Gee, I really feel guilty over this, and I can see why—it is a kind of conditioned reflex." I didn't have to feel stupid or neurotic, or put myself down for feeling that way.

One more suggestion. When you're feeling guilty over something that you feel is OK and when the situation is likely to occur often in the future, then deliberately do whatever it is you feel guilty about, as often as possible, and publicly affirm that you think it's OK. And if you can find other people who feel the same, talk with them about it to get their extra reinforcement. Eventually your guilt feelings will subside. For example, when I was young I was always told that it was wrong to miss church on Sunday. When I was a young adult I reasoned out that it was OK—the important thing was whether attending church made me a better person. But when I thought of missing church I still felt guilty. I examined the standard I was breaking, which gave rise to the guilt feelings, and decided it was a standard I no longer agreed with; then I accepted my guilty feelings as understandable; I shared them with my friends; and then I began publicly affirming my position and deliberately not going to church on Sunday for awhile. After a while I didn't feel guilty anymore, and became able to comfortably *choose* to attend church or not.

This system then, suggests 1) coming to some conclusions about your moral standards, 2) checking your guilt feelings against your standards to see whether they're productive or not, 3) if they're unproductive, accepting them anyway and defusing them, and then 4) deliberately doing whatever you feel guilty about and publicly affirming it and even reinforcing your feelings by talking with others who feel the same way. The system has worked for many people. It has worked for people who could never say no before without feeling guilty, it has worked for people who were afraid to be honest with their friends for fear of hurting their feelings, it has worked for gay people who couldn't accept their sexual orientation, and it has worked for people who have changed other behaviors from the patterns taught by their parents.

And it can work for you.

16

Liking Yourself

You have heard it said, "Thou shalt love thy neighbor as thyself." But a new commandment I give to you: "Thou shalt love thyself."

Do you love yourself? I'm not talking just about accepting yourself. After all, you could say, "I'm a pretty rotten and despicable person, but I accept myself that way." No, I'm talking about really liking what you accept. I'm talking about being able to look into your mirror in the morning and say, "You devil you;" or to every once in a while pat yourself on the back and say, "I am really a neat person. Boy, am I fun to be with. I'm glad to have me as a friend." *That* is liking yourself.

Now, liking yourself is not an all-or-nothing deal, as I mentioned in Chapter 7. The fact that you are alive means you've been taking care of your bodily needs enough to keep body and soul together—you like yourself enough to at least keep yourself alive. But if you like yourself only a little, then the love you try to give to others will lack the depth that it might otherwise convey. For example, the woman who thinks she isn't worth very much may compensate for her lack of self-love by trying to win the love of her husband and children and she may sacrifice of herself to do things for them. But it doesn't always feel good to get kindness when you know someone is giving it to you out of a feeling of obligation, or if it's a subtle form of manipulation; and so her gift of kindness may not be such a welcome gift after all. But if that woman really likes herself, then she won't need to make up for an incompleteness in herself by trying to win somebody's affection. Her love will be overflowing and her husband and children won't have to feel guilty in accepting her kindness because they'll know she didn't diminish herself to give it. Liking yourself makes liking others easier and more fun, and it makes it easier for people to receive your love.

Although self-esteem has many benefits, however, many of us don't like ourselves very much because we've been taught to be "humble" and not conceited. And besides, life seems easier if we don't. If we think of ourselves as incompetent and worthless, then we won't have to rise up to any challenges; we won't have to risk anything. When you have a low self-image, the world is more predictable because you believe you don't have the competence to do anything new. Life is pretty secure that way. *Or*, if you do try something new, you won't feel bad about failing. You can say, "Oh, I *knew* I wasn't good enough." It's handy to feel bad about yourself—it keeps you from having to really try anything risky.

There have been some interesting experiments with children that illustrate this. One study compared children who had self-confidence with those who didn't, in a ring-tossing game. A stake was set up for the rings to be tossed over, and the children were told that they could throw their ring from whatever position they wanted. Those with high self-confidence generally threw their rings from a reasonable distance away from the stake. Those with low self-confidence either stood right next to the stake so that no skill was needed to land their ring on it, or else they stood so far away from it that they couldn't possibly land their ring on the stake. That's the way we often act when we don't really trust ourselves to do anything right. We either put ourselves into easy, no-risk situations so that we *can't* fail, or else we put ourselves into situations where we are *bound* to fail. Either way, we haven't really risked anything, we haven't done anything that might put us into a new situation with new challenges. Life is pretty secure when you don't think very much of yourself. You pay for not liking yourself in having less exhilaration and zest in your life, but your reward is that you get to sail in a predictable boat that doesn't get rocked. People who don't like themselves very much come in two main varieties: self-effacing, or conceited. They either think they are worthless or else they think they are better than everyone else. The person who is always looking down his/her nose at other people, continually bragging, or putting other people down in order to raise her/himself up—that's a person who doesn't like self very much. If you have a low self-image, you may find that you over-exalt yourself so that you won't have to admit just how worthless you feel. If you have either an inferiority complex *or* a superiority complex, then you probably don't like yourself as much as you could.

Also, people who don't like themselves much tend to be either very selfish or over-generous. If you're stingy with your love, then you must be afraid of not having enough of it for yourself, so you keep all your gifts for yourself to fill your emptiness. Your selfishness is a way of calming your fear that no one will love you because you're not worthwhile. The extremely selfish person may *seem* to have self-love, and may do things for him/herself all the time. But the truth is that the selfish person doesn't really feel very good about self, or s/he wouldn't have to continually worry about hoarding strokes for him/herself.

Overly generous, overly kind people usually don't like themselves very much either. People who are always doing things for you and never letting you do anything for them, people who are continually kind and never show any negative feelings—these are people who either feel they are so worthless that they have to give and give to make up for it, or else they think that by doing things for others they can win their love, buy their love, because they don't have enough love of their own to satisfy their craving. There is a way to tell the difference between the person who is kind because he doesn't love himself and needs to compensate by doing things for others, and the person who is kind because she loves herself so much that it overflows in generosity to others. When you get kindness from people who like themselves, it feels good; it feels free. When you get kindness from people who don't like themselves, it doesn't feel so good. Either it feels like a manipulative thing — something to buy your love — and therefore not like a free gift at all. Or else it hurts to receive it because you know the other person doesn't really want to give but feels he or she has to give out of a sense of obligation. And who wants kindness from a martyr?

Perhaps you would like to like yourself more. Here are several suggestions for increasing your self-esteem. First, *take time out of every day*, or at least one period of time each week, *to do something for yourself.* What you do for yourself may involve other people or it may not; it could conceivably involve helping other people, if that really turns you on. But the important thing is that you do something that pleases *you*; it doesn't have to please anyone else. Taking time out for yourself will serve two functions: It will give you time to recharge your batteries and give you some respite from your maddening day. And — at least as importantly — it will show you that you consider yourself important enough to reserve time for. This may sound like a cart-before-the-horse type of thing, because you might expect a person to like him/herself first and *then* take time for self. But I'm suggesting that if you deliberately set aside time for yourself, you'll find yourself saying, "Gee, I must like myself to be giving me all this time," and you *will* gradually like yourself more and more!

Second suggestion: *Accept compliments.* When someone tells you that you look nice or that you're smart or that you did something beautiful, thank them. Don't say, "Oh no, I look awful," or "No, I'm so uninformed," or "That beautiful thing I did was by accident." If you deny compliments that way, you're either showing that you refuse to believe anything good about yourself, or else you're pushing the other person to compliment you again, or both. In either case you don't help your self-confidence much. So start accepting those compliments and saying to yourself, "Yeah, that's right: I *am* a pretty neat person." You're doing something nice for you *and* for the complimentor.

The third suggestion is related to the second one: *Start complimenting yourself.* Whenever you find yourself doing something neat or saying something profound or feeling or thinking or looking good, give yourself some praise. We are brought up in this society learning that you're never supposed to praise yourself—that's considered conceited. So we find ways to manipulate other people into giving us positive feedback instead of giving it to ourselves. You *are* a good person. Tell yourself that. You deserve to hear it. Praise yourself during the day and then perhaps at night make a list—either mental or written—of all the neat things you've done. If you've done awful things, then include those too, but for God's sake, forgive yourself!

Suggestion no. 4: *Pay attention to your body.* Now, your body may not seem significant. It's your spiritual essence that's important, right? Wrong. Your body is what you and other people see of you. It's a symbol of you, whether you consciously recognize that or not. If you can't relate positively to that ol' body of yours, then you probably can't relate positively with your self. You don't have to be beautiful or handsome or shapely or sexy-looking. You have, at the very least, an *interesting* body. Get in front of a mirror sometime and look at yourself, feel the texture of your skin, your hair. Talk to yourself in front of a mirror; smile and see just how nice you look when you smile. Sing a little song, do a little dance, appreciate your body, tune it up (re-read Chapter 12).

My fifth suggestion is that you *write yourself a letter occasionally.* Be honest in your letter, but be sure to tell yourself how worthwhile it is to have yourself as a friend.

> Dear Tony,
>   It's been a while since I've written you, and I just wanted to say hello and tell you that I really like

having you as my friend. You're so thoughtful and
kind, and you're funny too! You're clever, and you
write great books. I think you're generous,
sensitive, and really "alive." Your big nose is
distinctive, and I like the fuzzy feeling of your
beard. So long for now.

Suggestion no. 6: *Find someone that you can trust to
accept you, and share your feelings with that person.* It
should be a person that you can brag a little with and also
admit your weaknesses and feelings of inadequacy to. An
ideal person might be someone who is beginning to get to like
himself or herself better too—then you can both help each
other.

Seventh suggestion: *Use the relaxation exercise from
Chapter 10* with the section on increasing self-esteem (see
page 113).

And here's a radical suggestion, for those who just don't
believe they have anything to feel good about. *Write down or
say to yourself all the most awful things you can imagine
about yourself. And then exaggerate them.* Leave no stone
unturned in your search for evidence to condemn yourself.
Repeat over and over: "I'm a dirty, no-good..." Eventually,
even you will be able to stop yourself and say, "Hey, wait a
minute. I'm not that bad." And that's the beginning of liking
yourself—finding at least a few qualities that are either good
or at least not as bad as they might be. Then you can begin to
further develop those qualities you *do* like: do the good things
more often; be a person you like more often; try items one
through seven above each day. In the end, you'll find more
and more things to like about yourself, until you find that you
like yourself, period.

There's a word for what you get when you receive
affirmation of your worth—from yourself or from another. It's
"warm fuzzy"—a term from Transactional Analysis (T.A.),
the popular school of psychology and therapy that was

introduced to the American public in Eric Berne's book, *Games People Play*, and in Thomas Harris's book, *I'm OK, You're OK*. Warm fuzzies are positive strokes that people give to each other and to themselves. A warm fuzzy could be hugging someone. It could be holding your friend or spouse in your arms; putting your hand across someone's shoulder. A warm fuzzy could also be saying to someone, "Gee, you look nice," or "I think you're neat." It could be telling your friend, "I like you," and it could even be saying to yourself, "I'm a pretty neat person—I like myself." Warm fuzzies can be physical or verbal. Hugs, smiles, touches, words—all the ways we say, "I like you because you're a nice person to like."

Think for a moment about giving warm fuzzies. How many times have you felt good feelings about people or had nice thoughts, and you didn't tell them? Have you ever wondered why it is that we usually don't go up to someone out of the blue and say something complimentary? "If I say something nice she'll think I'm just flattering her." "He'll think I'm weird for telling him something good about himself for no reason, because it just isn't done." "He or she probably won't accept the compliment."

Well, it's true, people are so unaccustomed to hearing nice things about themselves and so brain-washed into believing they should be "humble" that they sometimes won't believe you're sincere, and they may not accept the compliment. But do it anyway. Tell people they look good when they do, tell them what they said was meaningful if it was for you, tell them you feel good being around them if it's true. The worst they can do is deny it and throw back the compliment. Even if they won't accept the stroke at the moment, they may think about it later and feel good that you said it. They may throw away your compliment because they don't want to appear conceited, but deep-down, people do like to hear that others consider them worthwhile. So tell them. Tell your kids. Tell your parents. Tell your spouse. Tell your friends. Tell them some of the good things you like about them to help them feel warm and fuzzy about themselves.

But there's one thing you shouldn't do. *Don't lie to make people feel good!* Unfortunately, in our society it has become customary in certain situations for people to say nice things by rote — as, for example, when you see someone with a new outfit on and you feel compelled to say, "What a nice dress that is," even though you think it looks terrible. Now I'm not suggesting that you say, "Gee, you look rotten today, Arlene," but you don't have to lie either. Little "white lies" aren't as harmless as some people think. Probably all of us have at one time or another said, "I love the way you're decorating your house," when we don't; "I got a lot out of what you said," when we didn't; or "It was really nice meeting you," when it really wasn't. Those well-intentioned lies make it easier for all of us to distrust people even when they give us a real compliment. "Oh, they're just saying that to be nice — they probably don't mean it." No wonder people throw back compliments. Too many compliments are fake.

Don't say something nice if you don't feel like it. Then as people get to know you and learn that you don't say nice things just to be nice, they will believe you when you *do* tell them something good about themselves. It may take some people a while to learn this, and they may throw back your warm fuzzies at first, but it's possible they'll think about it later.

If you're ready to give positive strokes, let me emphasize what I said about receiving them. You know, you probably throw away as many warm fuzzies as you let yourself receive. "Gee, Ellen, you look nice." "Oh, that's a switch. I usually look terrible."

"Eric, that was thoughtful of you to have me over." "Oh no, it wasn't any bother."

"Annie, you have such a keen mind." "Yeah, I'm a real genius, ha-ha-ha."

"John, I really like you." "Oh, yeah, well, you don't really see my bad side."

Some time ago I came to realize how often *I* deflected

compliments. I was afraid to accept people's good feelings about me. I kept thinking, "There's got to be a criticism somewhere." And if there wasn't I felt there would be if they only knew me better. If someone came to me and said, "Tony, I want to talk to you about something," my immediate feeling was: "Oh no, what's wrong now?" Sometimes the person told me good things, but I kept thinking it was a prelude to criticism and I anxiously waited through the good comments and said to myself: "When are they going to get to the bad part?" Sometimes there *was* no bad part, and I worried for nothing. But even if there was criticism, I still missed letting all those warm fuzzies seep in and help me feel good about myself. Sometimes I waded through compliments from 99 people, looking for a put-down, and then instead of feeling good about the 99 warm fuzzies, I let the criticism depress me.

When people do this, it's because they've picked up the message that they don't *deserve* too many compliments, they're too *bad* for that. They have also come to believe that worrying about all possible criticism will supposedly soften its blow when it happens. So they're always waiting for the bubble to burst. And they don't let compliments come through. Stop yourself before you throw them away or pass them off with a quick nod or thank-you. The next time someone communicates good feelings to you, let them seep in.

But go a step further. You don't have to wait for positive strokes to come your way. You can ask for them. When you want some warmth, ask your friend to hold you. Ask your spouse or your friend to tell you some good things about yourself. "Al, I'm feeling down, and I really want to hear some neat things about me. Tell me some of the reasons why you like me."

"Rose, I'm feeling so happy and good about myself and I'd like to hear about your love for me, one more time!"

Asking for warm fuzzies is difficult for most people. We've been taught to be humble, and we think it sounds bad to ask

someone to toot our horn for us. There isn't anything wrong
with asking people to express their real feelings for us!
There's nothing puffed-up in being honest about your actual
talents and qualities. If your friends are good friends, they'll
understand your asking for positive strokes. And they'll be
happy to give them to you. Actually, this is more honest than
the devious ways we often ask for strokes. Many of us get
people to stroke us by putting ourselves down first. "Oh, I'm
so stupid, I can't do anything right," we say, which prompts
others to answer, "Oh no, you're really smart."

"Boy, I'm a terrible person." "Oh no, how can you say
that? I think you're really nice."

This becomes a game. We're afraid to ask for warm fuzzies
outright, so we manipulate people into giving them to us, by
putting ourselves down. And because this works, we keep
doing it.

As I explained in Chapter 10, there are two problems with
this strategy. One is that, although you get the positive
stroke, you've given yourself a negative stroke in the process.
The second problem is that when you get someone to praise
you by putting yourself down first, you never know whether
they really mean their praise or whether they're just feeling
sorry for you. So their positive stroke may not even feel
genuine.

You don't need to weasel warm fuzzies from people. Just
tell them you want some. They'll probably enjoy giving them.

You know, I was once asked at a workshop to sit in the
center of the group and let each person in the circle take turns
telling me the things they liked about me. I was a little
embarrassed to be in the center of all this praise, but it felt
really good. I was floating on a cloud after that. I had started
the conference somewhat depressed. But all these people
reminded me of things about myself that I knew I could feel
good about, and I felt uplifted. I'd like to suggest the same
exercise for you. Get your family together, or your friends,
and go around the circle having each person say at least one
good thing about each other person. In families especially,

much of the conversation that goes on revolves around telling people what they didn't do right. Take the time to tell each other the things you like about each other too. It's OK to hear good things about yourself. It's OK to ask people to tell you all the things they like about you. We all like that feeling like the one you get when a dog wags its tail out of sheer joy at seeing you and licks your face to prove it. We all want warm fuzzies. So go ahead and ask for them.

And, of course, don't forget what I said about developing your own supply of warm fuzzies by giving compliments to yourself. This may sound strange, and I'll admit I had a hard time believing it myself at first, but it does feel good to hear good things about you from yourself. At the workshop I just mentioned, one of the group leaders suggested that I write myself a letter that evening and share it with the group in the morning. As I started writing down the things I liked about myself, I realized that there was a lot more good in me than I had ever stopped to consider before. I shared it with the group and they thought it was neat too. And now I take it out when I'm feeling down or when I just want to remind myself that I'm worthwhile. And, surprising as it may sound, it does feel good to hear praise from yourself, especially since you don't have to worry about it being flattery. There's no reason to consciously lie to yourself. So what you have is pure, honest praise, which can sometimes be more uplifting than the positive strokes you get from others. Once you've written your letter, by the way, share it with your friends—their affirmation will reinforce your own good feelings.

Some people may tell you, "Oh, writing yourself a letter is so gimmicky." So what if it's gimmicky? It works.

Another thing you may want to do is stand in front of a mirror, to symbolize an encounter with yourself, and say, "I am strong. I am good. I'm a neat person to have as a friend," or some other appropriate words. Of course, you have to believe it, at least intellectually. Your emotional acceptance of your strength and goodness will follow after practice. What have you got to lose—a minute in the day?

Sure, it's possible to take the suggestions in this chapter to the extreme. You could become a real boor to others by constantly praising and congratulating yourself. That's not at all what I'm encouraging for you. Instead, remember the *relationship* of those commandments I noted at the beginning of the chapter: "Thou shalt love thy neighbor *as thyself*;" and "Thou shalt love thyself." You can only be a genuinely loving and giving person *for others* if you are nurturing *yourself* by loving and giving to *you*.

You can make yourself a better, happier person: 1) Give warm fuzzies to others freely. 2) Don't throw them away when they come your way but accept them, let them seep in. 3) Ask for them when you want one. And 4) give them to yourself. You'll feel better about you. You will be less a victim of problem emotions like anxiety, fear, and depression. It will be easier to give of yourself to others. And you'll help *other* people feel good just to be around you.

Great way to be, eh?

Part Four:
YOU

I've been talking about you all along in this book. But now I want you to get some important knowledge about yourself. I want you to understand your phoniness, your little routines. *Not* so that you will feel bad about yourself. No, I want you to laugh about yourself. You and I are pretty funny people, you know, with our acts and secret fears and soap-opera lives. So read the next two chapters with a smile. The joke's on you. And on everybody else. But the neat thing is that you can be *in* on the joke.

And laugh a whole lot.

17

Who Are You?
[Really]

Who are you? Who are you really?

There are at least three parts to you: the person you're pretending to be; the person you're secretly afraid you are; and the person you really are.

The last part is the most important, but we get so involved in acting out the person we pretend to be, and so busy repressing the person we're secretly afraid we are, that we often don't get around to seeing what and who we actually are. Let us examine our parts and expose them so that we can see and achieve our real identity.

First—the person we pretend to be. You know, all of us have our little acts, the parts we play to make ourselves look good and impress people and get them to like and respect us. Some of us are such good actors that we even convince ourselves—"Gee, this isn't an act; this is the way I really am." Sometimes it takes an outside observer to see through our roles and expose them for us. In case you have no inkling of the act or acts you're playing, I'd like to catalog a few for you. See which ones fit you and allow yourself to accept that.

The first one is the nice-guy act or nice-woman act. If you're playing this part, then you're nice to people all the time, even if it kills you. "She's such a nice person," "What a nice guy he is," people say. This is the kind of person who goes around giving the shirt off his back to everyone. He likes to pay for the bill when people are out to eat and would rather *not* let other people be as nice as he is. This is the kind of person who believes she does good deeds for others simply out of kindness, compassion, and concern for her brothers and sisters. A person who rarely thinks of self. But the truth is, the nice guy or nice woman thinks a lot about self. She puts on the nice-person routine in order to have people respect her and say, "Oh, how selfless she is." Or to convince himself that he is a worthwhile person because he thinks he isn't worthwhile unless he's always helping others. It's an ego-booster. An act.

How about the stable act. "I'm stable. Like a rock, always there to hold things together. Nothing phases me." Only, beneath the rock-like exterior you may find ulcers, or headaches, or else a person whose real feelings never surface because they've been pushed down for so long. Underneath many stable acts is a person who is afraid.

And then there's Super-Mom and Super-Dad. The parents who *always* love their children and just can't do enough for them. They literally *can't* do enough for their children because the role of super-parent means they must achieve ever higher vistas of selflessness. You know it's an act when you find that you "have" to do it even when you don't want to.

Of course, there's the macho act. "I'm a man. I never cry. I could beat you up in a fight. I'm sexy and a great lover. None of this mushy emotionalism for me. If I could, I would chew tobacco and ride with a herd of cattle into Marlboro Country." For women there's the sweet-young-thing role. "O-o-oh. I just can't do anything for myself. I can't think for myself and I can't decide for myself. I need a big, strong man to help me. So I'll just sit here and act coy until one comes along."

There's the reasonable act. "I am rational. I always use my mind, my reason, to solve problems. I am unlike the masses with their superstitions and prejudices. I am not a slave to feelings like other people. (I'm a slave to my act!)"

There's the humility routine. "I guess I'm not very

bright." "Oh, yes you are!" say others. "I'm just not as competent as you are." "Oh, of course you are," say others. A humility act is easy to see through because it's obvious that the "humble" person is evaluating herself much too low according to objective standards. When someone has done an obviously good job and yet he says, "Oh no, it wasn't very good," then there is a game in operation. He knows it was good. But he downplays it anyway. Why? Why pretend you're worse than you are? It's an act either to get people to praise you more or else to let them know you're no threat and have them like you. The irony is that the super-humble person usually has no idea she's putting on an act. She thinks an act is when you try to impress people with how great you are. But, you see, telling people how low you are makes them think you're pretty great for being so humble, and it's just as much an act as arrogance.

There are other acts. The always-free-never-uptight act. The I - got - myself - completely - together - and - boy - do - I - feel - sorry - for - neurotic - you act. And here's a role that I often find myself falling into: "I am warm and sincere and genuine and authentic and human. I am just so real and so open to everyone." Nonsense! None of us are like that. This act is just as phoney as the other ones. Only, it's a little more subtle. It's called the I-don't-have-an-act act.

The best way to tell whether your behavior is genuine or an act is to look for ulterior motives—that is, reasons for your behavior that are beyond the self evident reasons. For example, in the I'm-a-loving-genuine-person act, there's more there than being loving—there's the wish to have people be impressed by how loving you are. This is obvious when a person deliberately lets people see how many good things she's doing. She really wants to say, "Look at me. Tell me I'm nice." That's the ulterior motive behind the supposedly loving motive.

If you are really honest with yourself you'll find that you're involved in at least one act. As I look through the list that I've given you, I find myself involved in almost every single one

(and more). Of course, much of our behavior has mixed
motives, so the things we do may be partly real and partly a
game to get others to like us.

Now, it's OK to have an act. Really! It's quite OK. After
all, you may not want to directly tell people that you're trying
to impress them and get them to like you, so an act may do it
for you. But at least recognize that it's an act. If you don't,
then you will be sure to suffer anxiety about the second part
of your personality. The first part of you, your act, is the
person you're pretending to be. The second part is the person
you're secretly afraid you are.

You can often get an indication of who you're afraid you are
by looking at who you're pretending to be. The macho act
often masks masculine fears. Arrogance masks insecurity.
The humble routine often hides a self-righteous pride in
one's own virtue — "I'm humble and I'm proud of it."
Super-Parent is often afraid that he or she is inadequate as a
loving mother or father and has to constantly prove adequacy
by measurable deeds — "There, I did another wonderful thing
for my child; I must be a good parent." And why do you think
people try to come across as very "together," non-uptight,
and open? Why does anyone need to convince others that
s/he doesn't have an act? Because the person is secretly
afraid that s/he isn't together and open. S/he's afraid s/he *is*
uptight and phoney.

Who are you secretly afraid you are? You can get an idea
by examining the little routine you put on. You can also get
an idea by looking at some of your more frightening dreams
and fantasies and compulsive thoughts. Someone says, "I
had this awful dream. I dreamt I killed my husband. Isn't that
terrible?" No, that's not so terrible. It may mean you have a
lot of hostility toward your husband. "Oh no, how awful."
No, not so awful. Pretty common. Does that mean you're a
bad person? No worse than the rest of us who feel hostility
toward other people sometimes. Does that mean you don't
love your husband? Not necessarily. You can love a person
and still hate him sometimes.

"But I have this fantasy with every new person I begin to get to know, that they're going to reject me." So, you're afraid you'll be rejected. Does this mean you're paranoid? No more paranoid than the rest of us who are afraid of this or that. Your fear of rejection probably also means you don't feel worthwhile enough in yourself—you're afraid that once people get to really know you, they'll back away.

Well, some of them will! (But so what?)

"I'm afraid that, deep inside, I'm really a very selfish person. I try to fake it, but I'm really self-centered." So what? So you're insecure. So you're selfish. So you're not together. So what? Does that mean life isn't worth living because you're not perfect?

Yes, you have an act, you have many acts. So you try to impress people and do things to get them to like you and you're not upfront about it. Fine. Join the human race.

And you know that person you're secretly afraid you are? Selfish, insecure, petty, arrogant, narrow-minded, uptight, hateful? You probably are those things. But a) that's nothing to be afraid of, and b) you also sometimes go the other way—you're sometimes kind, secure, open-minded, "together," and loving.

At a growth workshop a few years ago I came to some conclusions about my career. All this time I had been thinking that I became a minister because I have this great love and concern for people. That was the act I put on. And I must admit, it's a pretty good act—at times I almost convince myself. But my secret fear was that I'm not what my act says I am. At the workshop I was able to see through this act, this pretense, and also to admit the truth in my fear. Only, I realized that I didn't have to fear that truth. So I do good things in order to get people to like and respect me. And what greater way to accomplish that than the ministry? "Ministers are so good and caring. Especially the 'hip,' liberal ones like me, who are so friendly and open."

What an act! And here I get to stand up in front of my congregation Sunday after Sunday and say my piece. Oh, how many people would love to have that opportunity. But of course a minister doesn't stand behind the pulpit so he can be the center of attention. He's just there doing God's bidding (!). Don't you believe it!

Now, does that mean a person shouldn't be a minister or whatever because his or her motivation isn't pure? No. If you can do a decent job at whatever you do and enjoy it at the same time, why not? Neither you nor I have to do everything for the right reason. Just be glad that you do *some* things for the right reason—and you do, you know. Sometimes you are actually quite heroic and inspiring in the love you give. Sometimes you make sacrifices or take a stand that you know won't win you any friends or other rewards. Maybe that's only five percent of the time, but that is part of your nature too.

Rejoice for the things you do out of genuine love. *And*, rejoice for the things you do that help people even though you're doing them partly or wholly because you want to impress others. If you volunteer time or money to a project or cause or people, the project, the cause, the people are still helped by you regardless of your motivation. If you do good, then—no matter whether you did it to really *be* good or to merely *look* good—the fact remains that you *did* something good. And whoever is helped by your good deed probably won't care too much whether your sacrifice was a "pure" one or not!

So, regarding the person you're afraid you are, my advice is: accept it. The more you accept those parts of you that don't seem so nice, the less fearful they will appear. And the less you feel you have to hide that part of you, the more you will be able to see that there really is a heroic side to you too. Did you know that? Besides all your acts and your self-centeredness you have some really inspiring love for others. I don't care how little of it you think you have. You do have some. Self*less* love and self-*centered* love. That's a combination you can live with.

Regarding the person you're pretending to be, accept that

too. When you catch yourself in an act, admit it. At least to yourself. It's no great tragedy. When I catch myself putting on an act, I usually laugh to myself, "There I go again." When you realize everyone else has an act too, it's pretty funny. You may also find that being honest with others about your act can deepen your relationship, give others freedom to be honest too, and generally increase others' respect for you.

Of course, if you're honest about your act in order to have people respect you, then that's an act too. "Oh, she's so real, so honest," they will say. "She even admits it when she's *not* honest—that's how honest she is!" If you're honest about your act in order to get people to say that, you're doing a variation on the I-don't-have-an-act act; it's called the I-have-an-act-but-at-least-I'm-honest-about-it act. But you can admit that too!

Now, you may be thinking this is depressing. "First he tells me I'm pretending to be something I'm not; then he says I really *am* the things I'm afraid I am!"

Yes, that's true, but it's nothing to be depressed about. First of all, it's more funny than depressing—people working hard to become ministers or police or politicians or doctors or teachers or social workers or professors or parents or psychologists or entertainers or whatever else will project a good act for themselves. That's really funny. If you're still taking your act too seriously, then go to a Woody Allen film festival a few times and find out how funny you and the rest of the human race are. Once you can accept that, you will not only be able to laugh; you'll also be free to see that you have a heroic side too. You've been so busy trying to project a loving, "with it" act, and so busy trying to repress your fear that you aren't that, that you haven't been able to see that sometimes you really and truly are. You are actually a combination of fears, pretenses, and honest-to-goodness courage and love. So what if you're pretty heavy on the fearful, pretentious side? So what if you're not perfect? No one is. You are a combination of fears, pretenses, and honest-to-goodness courage and love.

And that's not such a bad combination.
Particularly if you can recognize and accept it.

18

How to Have Your Own Soap Opera

Yes, you can have your very own soap opera. No more daytime serials. Your everyday life can be just as melodramatic as "Love of Life" or "General Hospital." All you have to do is draw out small happenings in your life and elaborate every detail to make them loom large. Take dull events and talk about them as if they were world-shaking. Take the ordinary drama of your life and make it into a melodrama, and you'll have your very own "Days of Our Lives."

Of course, there are a number of plot lines to draw from. Pick the one that will fit your story best. There's the one called "Love of Martyrdom," for example. That's the story where you get to be the saintly sufferer. Here are some of the lines from this serial: "I tell you, I did more than my share to make our marriage work. *I* was thoughtful, generous, and kind. And then look at what happens." Or, "I've worked so hard. I gave my life's blood to that company. And all I got for my slave labor was arthritis and a gold watch." Here's a common parental soap opera, laughable only because it's so stereotypical: "I did everything for you kids. And did I ever ask for anything in return? And me with my health condition. Oh, how I've suffered."

Another good story is the rags-to-riches routine. And here's a good line from that script: "Why, when I was a boy, it wasn't as easy as it is today. We were so poor, I had to quit school so I could support my family. But I pulled myself up through hard work to get where I am today."

For a particularly poignant soap opera, try the one called "I Was a Failure." "I...I never made it in life. No one loved me. My parents rejected me. I was ugly. I was shy. Nobody ever gave me a break. Nothing I did turned out right. I was a failure." If you milk that story for all it's worth, you can make a real tear-jerker out of it. It also serves as a good excuse for being a failure today.

Frankly, this last one is just about my favorite soap opera. I love telling people about my childhood, with all the hardships I had to endure and the failures I had to cope with. But I get an even better story when I combine this one with the ever-popular plot of rags-to-riches. "Yes, I was rejected, and a failure. But look how far I've come." If I tell it right, my story can almost draw tears.

> When I was a child we were poor, and the other kids laughed at me because the clothes I wore were patched-up hand-me-downs.
>
> "Oh, Tony, I didn't know you were so poor."
>
> Well, it wasn't too bad. I had love, after all. But it's true that St. Vincent de Paul used to bring baskets of food to our house at Thanksgiving.
>
> "You're kidding."
>
> And I remember that at my graduation from eighth grade, one of the wealthier families in my school donated a suit for me to wear. It was the suit of one of the boys in my class, but he never said anything about it. I really liked it—it was the best suit I'd ever owned.
>
> "Oh, Tony, how touching."
>
> Of course, I felt set apart in other ways too. For example, I was never any good in sports, and the other boys made fun of me. I was always picked last to be on a team.
>
> "Oh, how awful."

I know.
"You must have felt so rejected and lonely."
I did. It was very painful.

And now for the rags-to-riches part.

"Gee, Tony, you're so put together, considering all you've been through."
Well, I guess I'm lucky to have come through it OK.
"I think it's just wonderful the way you've gotten yourself together. You're so healthy and well-adjusted."
Well, I like to think so.

Can't you just see that as the script in a B movie? Everything in this script is true. But it's a soap opera nonetheless.

There are other good variations on these story lines that you might want to use too. Like: "I can't help it—I came from a broken home"; "Nothing ever works out for me"; "You wouldn't *believe* what I've been through."

All of us have at least a few soap operas in our repertoire. Sometimes we make our whole life into one. Other times we just use a day's episode, as when we say, "Boy, what a day I've had."

If you don't think you have soap operas, then count the number of times you use the following phrases, which are usually introductions to another episode in the melodrama of your life: 1) Boy, what a day I've had. 2) I'm telling you... 3) You're not going to believe this... 4) When I was young... 5) Good Lord... 6) I don't believe it. 7) You mean to tell me...

Now, if you'd like to tell one of your soap operas, but you want to be asked to tell it, use one of these opening lines: 1) "Some people!" (That will prompt the other person to say, "What happened?") 2) Just grunt or say, "Hmmph." (The other person should respond, "What's wrong?") 3) "Don't

even ask me about my day. I don't want to talk about it."
(The other person will say, "That bad, huh?" And then you
can proceed to elaborate.) 4) Just roll your eyes or sigh. (Any
perceptive person should be moved to ask what's the matter.)

"I really don't want to talk about it," we say. Sometimes
it's true—we don't. Often we're *dying* to tell, and our
opening line manipulates the other person into asking, "But
why don't you want to talk about it?" We then may hold off
for a reasonable period of time and finally condescend to tell
our story. You see, deep inside us is the fear that the other
person won't think our concern is all that important. She or
he might think we're being melodramatic (which, of course,
we often are, because that's what soap operas are all about).
So we need to get the other person to beg to hear it. That way
the person will be committed to its importance. "Oh, it's
nothing," we say with a martyred look. Oh, but it's
everything—it's everything to the person who is really
committed to living a melodrama.

Now, before you start analyzing your own melodramas,
remember that there are two major possibilities for a soap
opera. Either it will a) contain one incredible event after
another, or b) contain relatively innocuous events that people
pretend are incredible. Consider the shows you see on TV.
Either you will find Jack having an affair with Betty, a former
prostitute, who is now dying of cancer (though she doesn't
know it) and whose brother is the homosexual doctor that
performed the abortion for Betty's kid sister who died of a
drug overdose after she discovered her divorced mother was
dating a fallen-away priest with leukemia. *Or*, Jack isn't
having an affair and no one is dying of anything (except
boredom), but the episodes go on and on anyway, drawing
the plot out so long that you can miss a week's shows and still
find that Jack and Betty are fighting about what color to paint
the bathroom. Incredible events, *or* trivial events that are
treated as if they are incredible.

A good example of the trivial was the scene in the movie
"Auntie Mame," where Mame's friends are talking about

the book she is writing to describe her life, and suddenly the girlfriend of Mame's nephew interrupts to tell *her* story. "*Well*," she says, "you could practically write a book about what happened to *me*." "Oh, really?" say the others. "Oh, *yes*. I was playing ping pong in this very important match and we lost the ball. Can you *believe* it?" Pause. "*Well*, we went to the storage room to get another ball and guess what? It was *locked!* It was ghastly. Just ghastly." And at first everyone just stares at her, as if to say, "And then what happened?"

Trivial events, but she felt they were worth writing a book about.

Now, it's true that some people do lead an incredible life while others live an uneventful existence. But most of *either* group will believe that their lives have a great deal of drama. You see, for many of us it doesn't matter how much happens in our life—we'll make a soap opera out of it anyway. When you're young, it's "Oh my *God*, I don't have enough money for the Prom." When you're a little older, it's "Oh my *God*, I don't have enough money to pay my doctor bills." When you're older still, it's "Oh my *God*, I don't have enough money to buy a swimming pool." It's all the same. If all of your major problems went away you'd make minor difficulties into major problems. You want *something* to sigh about, don't you?

To show you how relative our problems are, I'd like you to read the following statements out loud with as much drama as possible, and see if any one sounds more dramatic than the others:

"Would you believe, I was almost killed in a car accident yesterday!"

"Would you believe, my plane was an hour late!"

"Would you believe, I won $100,000 in a lottery contest!"

"Would you believe, I couldn't find the key to my car last night!"

"Would you believe, a flying saucer crew took me
aboard last night!"
"Would you believe, I brushed my teeth this morning
with Bryl Cream!"

It's all the same in our lives. Each one of these statements
is just as dramatic as we wish to make it. A moment ago I
made a distinction between soap operas in which incredible
things happen and the ones in which trivial things happen.
But in our actual lives the distinction fades because we'll
make a soap opera out of anything.

Not that I'm knocking soap operas. It's nice to have at least
a few stories to tell. They help us believe we're
important—we must be, after all, if such important things are
happening to us. They also get other people to pay attention
to us, which, again, helps us feel important. And they give us
something to talk about at cocktail parties. But it is good to
recognize them for what they are, for two reasons: First, if we
don't realize our stories are soap operas, we may carry some
around that are destructive. A psychologist I knew told of a
woman who came for counseling with her alcoholic husband.
As she told their story, it seemed she had been through pure
hell. After counseling her husband stopped drinking, but
then *she* became a nervous wreck. Some time later she
visited the psychologist again, and this time he couldn't help
noticing that she now looked refreshed. "You look good," the
counselor said. "How are things going?" "Well," she
answered calmly, "he's back to drinking again."

You see, she became a nervous wreck when her husband
took away her story of suffering. Now that he was drinking
again, she could play her role in "Love of Martyrdom."

If you're hanging on to a soap opera that keeps you from
being free, it would be well to recognize it for what it is. Once
you do, it will be more difficult to take it seriously and you'll
be able to let go of it eventually. Not that it's easy to do this.
Watch someone tell his story of failure some time and
observe how he relishes every detail. You'll see why it's hard

to give it up—especially when it offers an excuse for not doing anything in the present. Once you really see your story as a soap opera, you defuse its potential of locking you into destructive patterns.

The second reason for recognizing your melodramas for what they are is that you can then change your perspective on tragedy. You're in a car accident. "Oh my God, at least $500 worth of damage!" Yeah, and 10,000 people are dying today of starvation. And terrorists are holding hostages. And the world is threatened with a nuclear holocaust. And Betty Ann Windorpski went to work today without her lipstick! Can you imagine? You thought *you* had problems. What about poor Betty Ann?

I'm not saying you should be able to laugh away every problem. It's healthy to let yourself experience your anger, your hurting, and your frustration. But then go beyond it if you can. No matter what dramatic event is happening in your life, you can be sure there's a better soap opera taking place somewhere else.

Look at your life. So you have failed. So you're an alcoholic. So you attempted suicide. So you've been rejected. So your close friend died. So, gee willickers, Mrs. Olson, but you just can't make good coffee.

So what? Life goes on.

Tell your story, yes. But don't let yourself be molded or locked in by it. Since life is a soap opera, there's no reason in the world why you can't rewrite the script from time to time.

By the way, don't worry if your life doesn't sound as melodramatic as other people's. It's not the events that matter so much—it's how you tell them.

One more by-the-way: I *did* once brush my teeth with Bryl Cream.

Part Five:
MAKING LIFE
THE BEST
POSSIBLE GAME

It is a game, you know. A game with chips. I told you all about that in Chapter 11. Now I want you to see how to have the best life-game possible, by drawing from what I've said in all the chapters.

19

Making Life the Best
Possible Game

First, I want you to understand a few things about your life
so that you'll be in the right frame of mind to play it well.
The first thing has to do with freedom. I've been talking
about that throughout this whole book, but I want to
underline it now so that you don't forget it: Not only are you
free now to make choices...but you *have* been making choices
all along, every day, every minute. That's right. You can
never be *un*free—at least not ultimately—because even
being that, represents a choice. And a choice implies
freedom.

Look at all the choices you've made just since this morning.
There was the decision to get out of bed, for one thing. The
decision to brush your teeth, maybe eat something. The
decision about what clothes to wear, and even the decision to
put them on. The choice to read this book. The choice to
continue reading this book. Do you see? Every next word you
read is a choice to go on. The sentence you're reading *right*
now represents a choice. I'm not *making* you read this
sentence. Or *this* sentence. Or *this* one. *You* are choosing to
do that. Everything you do represents a decision to do one act
and not do other possible ones. Even the things you do by
habit, like eating food when you're hungry. "But I have to
eat," you say. "Otherwise I'd die." Precisely. Eating is a
decision to live. "But I never decided to live." Ah, but you
did, and you do. If you decided to do nothing, you would

starve. But you have decided to do things. Every time you eat or drink or take a vitamin tablet or turn your heater on in the winter, you are in effect deciding that life, so far at least, is worth it.

What I'm saying here may seem obvious or even trivial. But I want you to see that you do indeed have choices, that everything you do represents a choice—a decision to do this, or at least a decision *not* to do something else. If you can understand that you do have choices, then you will understand that you have freedom—because freedom means the ability to choose. You may not have as much of it as you'd like, because you may not have as many alternatives as you would like to choose from. For example, as I've said before, you're not free to fly to Mars today, no matter how much you want to. But you are free to talk to people today or not, have a cup of coffee or not, scratch your nose or not, read what I'm saying right now or not, make some big changes in your life or not—you are free to live today or not.

"Oh, but I'm not free. I don't have choices anymore. My spouse has become bitter, and I never chose that." "I've had to work hard all my life for the little I got, and I didn't choose that." Perhaps you didn't choose to have an unloving spouse or to be poor. But you did decide how you would react to these, consciously or unconsciously. And of course, no one ever said you could choose *anything*—even the richest person on earth can't fly to Mars—yet—but you do make choices out of the alternatives open to you. There are always alternatives—not as many as you might like, of course, but they are there. Some people act as if they are helpless pawns in the hand of fate. "Oh, what could I do? There was no choice." Yes there was. "But Mary Ellen called up and talked my ear off for hours, and there was no way to stop her." You could have hung up. "But that would have made her angry at me." OK, and you didn't want that so you decided against it. But you still had that choice.

I know of a woman whose husband has progressed steadily into alcoholism until he is now little more than a vegetable.

She and her children are very bitter now. She didn't make the decision for him to be alcoholic. But she did decide not to throw him out when the problem first became very serious. Instead of saying, "You go for help or you get out," she decided to try to hide the problem, to ignore it, to pretend it away, hope it away. "But she couldn't just throw him out," people said. Yes, she could have. "But her religion said marriage is forever." She could have re-evaluated her religion. "But people would have thought she was terrible." Maybe. But she could have chosen other than as she chose. Even now she can decide. She may not have many wonderful alternatives to choose from, but she does have alternatives. She—and you and I—may not be able to choose how everything will happen to us, but we can choose what to do about the things that happen to us, how to react to them.

Actually, even some of the things that "happen" to us are at least partly our choice. For example, I had an accident one evening, driving in the rain, when my car slipped on the road and crashed into the cement highway divider. Funny—we usually use the word "accident" to mean something that happens by chance, something that takes place without human design or reasoning (as when we say, "I discovered this by accident"—that is, without planning to). And we refer to automobile crashes as accidents because of course nobody *plans* to run into cement dividers.

But this car accident (and probably most car accidents) didn't just "happen." *I* chose it, *I* caused it — at least partially. That's a sobering thing to admit to oneself, but it's true. I did at least four things to contribute to the car crash: 1) I drove a car with old tires (which, although not threadbare, did not provide much traction); 2) I drove on a wet road (which is usually what you get when it rains); 3) I drove faster than I might have, considering the weather conditions; and 4) I drove, period. (Remember, every time you get into a car you take a risk.) By eliminating any one of these I might *not* have had the accident. So in a very real sense I *chose* what happened, to some degree. There is a risk involved in everything you do. (And when you don't *know* what the risk is, then *that's* a risk too.)

No excuses for ignorance. No excuses, period. Start taking responsibility for your life—even (and especially) for the things that seem to just "happen" to you. If you look carefully you'll usually find that you could have done things to prevent them. The fact that you *didn't* do those things shows that you chose to let whatever happen happen.

Now it's true that in the case of my crash I didn't consciously choose (or want—which is the same thing) to crash. But I apparently didn't want to not crash, enough to take precautions. So my want to not crash was less than my want to not bother taking precautions. In other words, I wanted to take the chance of having an accident more than I wanted to go to the trouble of getting better tires, driving slower, or not driving at all. I *chose* that. Which just goes to show how much or how little I valued my life.

Why am I telling you that everything you do or don't do represents a choice? I'm telling you this because a) it's good for you to know that you are free—not free to do *anything*, but free to choose from among the alternatives open to you; and b) it's good for you to know *what* you've chosen. If you ate anything today, then you've chosen to live. If something bad happened to you, there's a good chance you had something to do with letting it happen. If you looked in the mirror this morning, then you've decided that you are important—at least important enough to look at. If you said something kind to someone today, then you've chosen to love. Maybe just a little. But even a little choice is a choice.

And part of a challenge. Do you know what a challenge is? It's a difficulty that you want to solve. It's what you need to make life an interesting, fun game.

Do you know what a problem is? It's the same thing as a challenge—it's a difficulty—only we often don't want to solve it so we don't let it be part of our game.

Amazing, isn't it? People want challenges. They *don't* want problems. But the only difference between those things they want and the ones they don't want is that they look at the challenges with a positive attitude and the problems with a negative one. Challenges and problems are the same thing—*you're* what distinguishes them from each other because you're the one who decides whether you want to enjoy solving them or hate solving them.

Let me say it again: There are two kinds of difficulties in this world: problems, and challenges. A problem is a difficulty that usually comes in this form: "Oh no, what am I going to do? Gee, I don't know, what *am* I going to do? Boy, I don't know; there's not much I *can* do. Yeah, I know, so what am I going to do?" In other words, a problem is a difficulty which—to anyone else at least—gets boring after a while. "Uh-oh. Here comes Edith with her 'problem.'"

A challenge, on the other hand, is a difficulty that is fun, exciting. We live for challenges. We actively seek out difficulties that are challenging because we enjoy trying to solve them. The first people to climb Mount Everest knew it would be difficult, but that was the excitement of it. It was a challenge to them. Imagine what it would be like to change the challenge of mountain climbing into a problem. "Hey, men, we've got this mountain to climb." "Oh no, how are we going to do *that?*" "Gee, I don't know; no one's ever done it before." "Oh, that's just great. Then what are we going to do?" "Boy, I don't know, there's not much we *can* do." "Yeah, I know, so what are we going to do?"

Notice how quickly the difficulty got boring when it moved from "challenge" to "problem"? As you can see, the same difficulty can be a problem for one person and a challenge for another. That's because problems and challenges don't exist "out there"—they're in *your* head.

We all want difficulties in our lives—that is, we all want things that are hard to do, that take effort and planning, and maybe are even gruelling. We all want difficulties so that life isn't boring. Why do people have children? Why do people knock themselves out to play sports? They don't *have* to play tennis or swim or water-ski. They knock themselves out doing these things because they *want* to. People who climb mountains don't do it because they *have* to—people *choose* difficult things to do.

Now, life has no shortage of difficulties. If you don't have enough of them in your personal life, then look at the world—there are plenty there to occupy your time and energy. What you and I should do is change some of our problem difficulties into challenging difficulties. That is, we need to take some of the difficulties in our lives over which we've been moaning and groaning and saying "What am I going to do? Gee, I don't know, what *am* I going to do?"—and change them into difficulties that we actively choose to solve, even with exhilaration.

Now, you may be saying to yourself, "Change my problems into challenges? How can I do that? Gee, I don't know, how *can* I do that?" You see, you're already making the transformation of problem-to-challenge a problem, instead of making the transformation of problem-to-challenge a challenge.

"Oh no, I just can't live with the changes coming in my life." You can change that too: "There are changes in my life, and I'm going to work through them and live through them, and do a good job at both." You can transform "Oh no, the world is in such a terrible mess" to: "The world's in a mess and I accept the challenge of doing my bit to make it less of a mess." You can transform "Gee, I feel so bad about myself, so worthless and hopeless" to: "I have bad feelings about myself and I'm going to do specific things to change that."

A large part of changing a *problem* difficulty into a *challenging* difficulty is to simply change your way of looking at the difficulty. The power is within you—of course! It's how you choose to look at life and deal with it. You can either go around complaining that rosebushes have thorns—or else you can rejoice that some thornbushes have roses! They're the same thing. *You're* the one with the power to see them differently.

The same is true with many other circumstances in life. I have seen this demonstrated in people I've worked with, time and time again. For example, I sometimes ask a group of people to write down one word to describe this person: "Jane does things by herself, spends most of her time alone, and doesn't do much with other people." What word would *you* pick to describe Jane? (Think of one before reading the next paragraph.)

* * * * * * * * * * * *

Was your word a positive one or negative? You know, some people call Jane "lonely" or "unhappy." Others use "self-reliant" or another positive term to describe her. As with *difficulties*, and whether you consider them challenges or problems, it all depends on your point of view.

Here's another example. If I told you to give me one word for a life in which nothing much changes, most things staying the same—what word would you pick?

Did you know that when a group of people is given this exercise, normally some write "boring" and others say "peaceful"?

Suppose I asked you to give me one word for "not having one set of circumstances put on you." What would your word be?

Did you know that some people call this freedom?

Others call it insecurity!

Take a look at your life from both sides now and decide whether you'll see:

> *aloneness* as being independent, being myself, being self-reliant...or being lonely
> *togetherness* as warm and loving...or limiting and encroaching
> *sameness* as peaceful...or boring
> *change* as exciting...or frightening
> *indeterminacy* as wonderful freedom...or terrible

insecurity
life's difficulties as challenges...or (groan) problems
and *life itself* as a game...or an ordeal.

If you decide to let life be a game and to let yourself play
(and play well), then here's a system for the best game
possible. Just make the following diagram your gameboard.

	which you can change	which you can't change
People, things, events outside of you that are problematic	**A**	**B**
Your problem feelings	**C**	**D**
Things you're doing or not doing that are problematic	**A**	**B**
Thoughts, beliefs, or attitudes you hold that are problematic	**E**	**F**
You or aspects of you that you find problematic	**G**	**H**

And everytime you find yourself landing in one of these life spaces, whether it's feelings, actions, events, whatever, and whether these can be changed or not changed—then pick up the card corresponding to the space and follow the instructions. You'll have the best game ever!

Here are the cards:

A	**B**
Well, change them. Just decide to, and then do it. Make sure that whatever you decide to do is specific, rather than general, so that you'll know whether you've accomplished your goals or not. And if you end up not doing anything to change whatever is bothering you, then you learn something: You didn't really want to change anything after all (at least not as much as you wanted to not bother). In this case, go to **B**.	OK. What is, is. Is your moaning and groaning going to do anything to change things? Nope. So accept the fact that here's a chip you don't have. By trying to play with it, you're taking time away from the game. Why do that? Just let it be and get on with the rest of your life. (If you're having problem feelings associated with this, then go to **C**.)

C

Here are ways to dissipate problem feelings, like anger, fear, or depression: gradual desensitization, through the relaxation exercise; watching others who model appropriate emotional responses; using I-Messages; just avoiding situations that elicit bad feelings; practicing responding without the bad feelings; implosive method (going through your feelings over and over until they bore you); increasing your self-esteem (see Chapter 16 for specific suggestions); frequent practice of the relaxation exercise (see pages 106-107); Gestalt method (the two-chair technique); examining your feelings intensely; examining the "causes" of your feelings; and changing the beliefs or thoughts you hold which help you feel bad. For detail on these methods, see Chapter 14. (For specific suggestions on hostility, see Chapter 13; on guilt feelings, Chapter 14; and for rejection, pages 166-170.) And don't forget the important effects of your physical condition on how you feel emotionally! (Re-read Chapter 12.)

D

Are you *sure* you can't change your feelings? Or is it that you just don't want to bother?

Well, either way, just accept them, then, as one of the obstacles life has given you. Nobody ever promised you life would be perfect. No one ever said you'd be happy all the time. So accept your problem feelings and just live through them. Time generally blunts their edge eventually anyway.

Don't believe there's something wrong with you for feeling the way you do, by the way. Feelings are generally conditioned responses. Many of these responses are dumb or inappropriate, but that's just the way the human computer works. For God's sake, don't go blaming *yourself* for having human equipment. That's just the way it is, that's all. Meanwhile, why not get some things done that don't need too much concentration or creativity, like cleaning or other perfunctory tasks? That way you'll at least have some things accomplished by the time you run through your feelings. That in itself may speed up the process of dissipation.

Also, remind yourself that you are a good person. You are, you know. Tell yourself that. Coming from you, it ought to count for something.

E

What you've got to do here is dispute those thoughts, beliefs, or attitudes. Talk to yourself, argue with yourself. Show yourself the irrationality of thinking the way you do. With some practice you, reasoning creature that you are, will convince yourself that things don't have to be as awful as you sometimes let them be. In fact, most things just *are—we* put labels of "wonderful" and "awful" on them. Once you see that the *labeler* (that's you) is the one who has the power, and not the labels themselves, then your thoughts, beliefs, and attitudes will change accordingly—and, with a little reminding from time to time, won't get in the way of happy, productive living.

F

The only thoughts, beliefs, or attitudes that you *can't* change are the ones that are true and reasonable.

Suppose you believe that you can't trust your child (or friend or spouse) to be responsible. And you want to change that belief, because it would be nice to be able to trust. Well, if this person has broken your trust, you can't make yourself believe s/he is trustworthy when you know s/he isn't. (And even if it were possible to do this, it would still be pretty dumb. Some people, by the way, use this line, "Trust me," as a guilt inducer—as if there's something wrong with *you* for not being willing to be naive, and as if belief were simply an act of the will. Crazy.)

OK, so those are beliefs you can't change (and shouldn't change) because they're true. But the ones that "cause" your problem feelings are usually not reasonable. And they *can* be changed. So if that's what you're dealing with, go back to E.

G

You are not a static thing. You're an ongoing process. So when you say you want to change you, or change certain aspects of you, all you're saying is that you want to think, act, or feel differently in the future. True, you can't change the past. It already happened. But you *can* decide to do things differently in the future. And that's all anyone can mean when s/he says s/he wants to change him/herself. (Because there isn't any other "you" around.) Thinking differently and acting differently are very simple. You just do them. And if you don't, that's only because you don't really *want* to change the way you think or act. And if that's true, you shouldn't really be reading this card.

Changing your feelings usually takes more than an act of the will, but it too is possible. (See C for the list of methods for this.)

Now, if you want to honestly change the way you will be in the future, then come to grips with your present and past pretenses (acts), your secret fears (don't let them be secret anymore), and what you really are. Accept all of that. Accept your soap operas too. *Then* you will be in a position to decide what you want to change (if anything).

You just may decide to keep yourself pretty much the way you are. (I think that's neat.) You just may decide to do a pretty extensive overhaul. (I think that's neat.) Either is fine. Either is neat. Either is powerful.

H

OK, so there are some things about you that you don't like which either you can't change or you don't want to go through the hassle of changing. So whoever said you had to be the perfect human being? There will *always* be aspects of your personality you may not like. Always—no matter how much you improve. So even if you were to change some parts that you don't like now, you'd *never* get to the point where you liked everything about yourself. Since you're *always* going to have some not-so-neat aspects to your personality, why make it a problem now?

You're OK just the way you are. You're surviving, aren't you? Well, give yourself a hand for *that!*

Now that you've looked the cards over, store them somewhere. In your head. On your bookshelf. Wherever. And just know that life can be a pretty good game for you once you realize that you have the power to handle it, instead of letting it handle you. Of course, "it" never *really* handles you. When we say that it does, we simply mean that *you* are handling you in an ineffective way. Because you're not willing to be clear about what you want or don't want, and about what chips you have or don't have. In that case you're abdicating your power. (And only *you* have the power to do that—no one else can take your power away from you.)

You also have the power to gain back your power, which is what I've been saying in a hundred different ways since page one. Nice, huh? You've got it. And since it sounds so nice together, with a kind of rhythm, you can make this a slogan of sorts, to chant for yourself now and again—just to remind you about you:

I have the power...to handle my world
instead of letting it handle me.
(Right on.)
I have the power...to handle my world
instead of letting it handle me.
(That's right.)
I have the power...to handle my world
instead of letting it handle me.
(You've got it.)
Etc.

Keep saying it. Keep believing it. And keep being it and doing it. You, powerful, you. *That's* what is. You'd better believe it! And TRUST YOURSELF!

SUGGESTIONS FOR FURTHER READING

You may be interested in pursuing particular areas suggested in this book. Here is a list of materials that you may find helpful as supplementary reading. I've listed them by chapter, but some apply to several of the topics we've covered.

FOR CHAPTER ONE: "What Is, Is"

Ellis, Albert, and Harper, R.A., *A New Guide to Rational Living*. Englewood Cliffs, New Jersey: Prentice-Hall, and Hollywood: Wilshire Books, 1975.
In this and his many other books, Albert Ellis, the founder of Rational Emotive Therapy, suggests that people can get rid of a lot of their problems by discarding "irrational beliefs." (See Chapter 14 of this book for further discussion of this approach.) One of the beliefs Ellis suggests we should discard is the belief that life must be fair, or that life should be good (meaning easy). He has humorous names for the common unwillingness to accept life as it is — "awfulizing" (making things seem worse than they are) or "can't-stand-it-itis."

Frankl, Victor E. *Man's Search for Meaning: An Introduction to Logotherapy*. Boston: Beacon Press, 1959.
I recommend this book not for its psychological theory particularly, but for its witness to the possibility of finding a meaningful, fulfilling life despite "unbearable" life situations. Written by a psychotherapist who survived a Nazi concentration camp, this little book (already a classic) shows how to accept those things you can't change in life, with serenity — and it does so simply by presenting the author's own personal life and witness, his transformation of evil into good, suffering into meaning. You will also see how much you have to be grateful for when you read this book, through the contrast it presents to your own life (so it serves as excellent supplemental reading to Chapter 2 as well).

Kaufman, Barry Neil, *To Love Is to Be Happy With*. New York: Fawcett-Crest, 1977.
"The difference between a flower and a weed is a judgment." Yes,

it's in you—in how you look at things. This is an excellent book for helping you understand this.

FOR CHAPTER TWO: "The Lost Coin"

Frankl, Victor E. *Man's Search for Meaning.* (See above suggestions for Chapter 1.)

Keller, Helen, *The Story of My Life.* Garden City, New York: Doubleday and Company, Inc., 1902.
It's a beautiful story. And it should get you to stop and think about how much you take for granted. Here's a woman who had much less than you—but knew how to be grateful for it anyway. Helen Keller—a living demonstration of the fact that you can create most of your own happiness, regardless of the outside "facts," through your own attitudes about life.

Keller, Helen, "Three Days to See."

Link, Mark, *In the Stillness Is the Dancing.* Niles, Illinois: Argus Communications, 1972.
This book is a collection of humanistic and religious quotations and photographs, many of them focussing on life's joy and wonder.

FOR CHAPTER THREE: "I Need, I Have to, I Don't Have the Time"

Ellis and Harper, *A New Guide to Rational Living.* (See above suggestions for Chapter 1.)
Although their position does not go as far as mine does in critiquing needs, Ellis and Harper rather clearly demonstrate the unreasonableness of most of our needs and have-to's. It is irrational, they note, to really believe that we *need* approval (*have to* have it) or need to have people love us. Since a need or a have-to can also be called a "must," they humorously refer to our creating all these needs and musts as "musturbation."

Kaufman, Barry Neil, *To Love Is to Be Happy With*. (See above suggestions for Chapter 1.)

FOR CHAPTER FOUR: "I Can't, But"

Satir, Virginia, *Making Contact*. Millbrae, California: Celestial Arts, 1976.
This little book makes a good complement to this chapter and the preceding ones.

(See also the resources suggested for Chapters 1-3 above.)

FOR CHAPTER FIVE: "Money"

There are lots of books on money. Just go to the card catalogue at your local library and look under "Money" to find the general area, and you'll find shelves and shelves of books on the subject. There are, as far as I can tell, three main types of them. 1) There are the books that tell you factually about what money is and how it works. 2) There are the books that give you advice on how to get the most out of the money you have and/or earn more of it. And 3) there are the books that offer you grandiose promises of wealth through positive thinking or some other simple scheme. (One such, on the shelf at my local library, is *Anyone Can Make a Million Dollars*.)

The problem with Category No. 1 is that most books of this type aren't written for the layperson. However, here are a few books about money and economics that are fairly easy to understand:

Morgan, E. Victor, *A History of Money*. Baltimore, Maryland: Penguin Books, 1965.

Ritter, Lawrence S., and Silber, William L. *Principles of Money, Banking and Financial Markets*. New York: Basic Books, Inc., 1977.

Samuelson, Paul A. *Economics: An Introductory Analysis*. New York, St. Louis, San Francisco, Toronto, London, Sydney: McGraw-Hill Book Company, 1976 (10th edition).

Two of the more popular books in Category No. 2 are listed below. Although I don't think they go far enough in suggesting that *you* have the power to determine the worth of things (and of you!) apart from money, they do offer some practical financial advice, so I've included them here.

Nelson, Paula, *The Joy of Money: The Guide to Women's Financial Freedom.* New York: Stein and Day, Publishers, 1975.

Porter, Sylvia, *Sylvia Porter's Money Book.* New York: Doubleday, 1975 (Paperback edition: Avon, 1976).

I have nothing to suggest for Category 3, for two reasons. First of all, I think many of the "think rich" and "how to make a bundle" books are deceptive in their simplicity. Most people just can't become rich overnight, and it is wrong to promise (or appear to promise) such "success." My second problem with books of Category 3 is that they reinforce the myth that having lots of money brings happiness (and "success"). In other words, while the approach of No. 3 books is that "You have the power to become rich (and therefore happy)"—the approach of Chapter 5 (and of this whole book) is that "You have the power to become happier—regardless of what money you do or don't have."

FOR CHAPTER SIX: "What Do You Want?"

Simon, Sidney B., Howe, Leland W., and Kirschenbaum, Howard, *Values Clarification: A Handbook of Practical Strategies for Teachers and Students.* New York: Hart Publishing Company, Inc., 1972.
This is the classic work on values clarification—the one that started it all. Although this book was written originally for use in the classroom, many of the exercises here can be used by the general reader to help you discover just what things are important to you, what your goals are, and what you want out of life. The authors don't tell you the answers to any of these questions—they merely suggest ways for you (by yourself or with others) to ask them yourself (and answer them!). Some of the more relevant (to this chapter) strategies in this book are: "Twenty Things You Love to Do"; "Rank Order"; "Value Survey" (based on the work of Milton

Rokeach); "Getting Started"; "The Pie of Life"; "Life Line"; "Epitaph"; "Obituary"; "Two Ideal Days"; "Life Inventory"; "Self Contracts"; "How Would Your Life Be Different?"; "What's in Your Wallet?"; "The Miracle Workers"; "Ways to Live"; "Ready for Summer"; and "The Suitcase Strategy."

FOR CHAPTER SEVEN: "How to Get Things Done That You've Been Putting Off"

Glasser, William, *Reality Therapy: A New Approch to Psychiatry.* New York: Harper and Row Publishers, Inc., 1965.
Although I disagree with some of Dr. Glasser's philosophy (for example he says people *need* to be loved and *need* to feel worthwhile to others, and he also seems to take a somewhat moralistic, or "preachy," position regarding values and decision-making), still the idea of taking responsibility for your life and your actions is one I heartily endorse. This particular book, by the way, is the classic exposition of the principles of Reality Therapy. Dr. Glasser was among the first to popularize the idea of the contract in psychotherapy—that is, he has his clients sign a "contract" that they will do such-and-such before the next therapy session and he accepts no excuses for not fulfilling it. In Chapter 7 I have suggested that the reader can contract with him/herself to do the same thing.

For a shorter exposition of Reality Therapy, see *Modern Therapies*, by Binder, Binder, and Rimland (listed with resources for Chapter 14 below.)

Lakein, Alan, *How to Get Control of Your Time and Your Life.* New York: Peter H. Wyden, Inc., 1973.
Some of the suggestions in this book may seem a little mechanical, but the book really does have some great ideas for getting more done in less time. Try it!

FOR CHAPTER NINE: "Stop Being Manipulated"

Alberti, Robert, ed., *Assertiveness: Innovations, Applications, Issues.* San Luis Obispo, California: Impact Publishers, Inc., 1977.

This book is a collection of short essays on various aspects of assertive training by leaders in the field—written in a very readable style and with many practical, useful suggestions. It is written *primarily* for professional trainers and therapists.

Alberti, Robert, and Emmons, Michael, *Your Perfect Right.* San Luis Obispo, California: Impact Publishers, Inc., 1970, 1974, 1978.
At the time of this writing there have been at least 20 books written on assertive training, but this is the one that opened up the field and started the "assertive movement." This very readable little book not only talks about verbal responses you can make to avoid manipulation—it explains how to practice assertiveness so that you can make it a natural part of your behavior.

Cotler, Sherwin B., and Guerra, Julio J., *Assertion Training: A Humanistic-Behavioral Guide to Self-Dignity.* Champaign, Illinois: Research Press Company, 1976.
Another practical book on improving assertive skills.

FOR CHAPTER TEN: "What Taoism Can Teach You About Doing Without Doing"

Bloomfield, Harold; Cain, Michael Peter; and Jaffe, Dennis T., *TM; Discovering Inner Energy and Overcoming Stress.* New York: Dell Publishing Company, Inc., 1975.
Transcendental Meditation, or TM, has become one of the most popular forms of the relaxation exercise, and this book explains it in more detail than I have (though I don't think the explanation is necessary in order to do it well). (See also Adam Smith's *Powers of Mind*, below, for a humorous but fairly thorough excursion through the realm of the new psychologies and techniques, including TM.)

Frederick, Carl, *est: Playing the Game the New Way.* New York: Dell Publishing Company, Inc., 1974.
Although this book is not specifically about using Taoist principles, and although I think it overemphasizes the power of the self to "create" reality, it does contain a number of good ideas, among them the advice to "give up being right" (in Chapter 4: "How to Get All the Cheese in Life," or "How Unreasonable Can You

Be?''), which is one of the suggestions I make in Chapter 10 of this book.

Patton, Kenneth L., *The Way for This Journey*. Ridgewood, New Jersey: Meeting House Press, 1976.
This little book is a quite readable collection of writings from Eastern religions, namely, Confucianism, Buddhism (including Zen), and Taoism. It's delightful.

Smith, Huston, *The Religions of Man*. New York: Harper and Row, Publishers, 1958.
This is still a quite popular introduction to the great world religions. It is simple, brief, easy to understand, but not shallow.

Waley, Arthur, *Three Ways of Thought in Ancient China*. Garden City, New York: Doubleday, 1956.

Welch, Holmes, *Taoism: The Parting of the Way*. Boston: Beacon Press, 1965.
Both of these books explain the basic philosophy of Taoism. For a shorter but very clear exposition of Taoism read Chapter 5 of Smith's *The Religions of Man* (see above).

FOR CHAPTER ELEVEN: "Working with the Chips You Have"

Kaufman, Barry Neil, *To Love Is to Be Happy With*. (See above suggestions for Chapter 1.)

(See also the other sources suggested for Chapter 1 of this book.)

FOR CHAPTER TWELVE: "Trusting and Tuning-up Your Body"

Ardell, Donald B., *High Level Wellness: An Alternative to Doctors, Drugs, and Disease*. Emmaus, Pennsylvania: Rodale Press, 1977.
The author suggests psychological *and* physical ways to increase well-being, and he covers a good many areas in both disciplines, noting research findings where applicable.

Berkeley Holistic Health Center (Ed.), *Holistic Health Handbook*, Berkeley, California: And/Or Press, P.O. Box 2246, Berkeley 94702, 1978.

Count Your Calories. Dell Purse Book #1532. New York: Dell Publishing Company, Inc., 1963.
This is a tiny booklet that you can keep in your back pocket or your purse for easy reference—over 2,000 foods listed.

Linde, Shirley, *The Whole Health Catalogue: How to Stay Well—Cheaper*. New York: Rawson Associates Publishers, Inc., 1977.
This book covers more than Dr. Ulene's book (see below), but, like all catalogues, in less detail. It's great as a resource book—just look in the Table of Contents or the Index for the health area you're interested in, and Ms. Linde has the pertinent facts waiting for you on the appropriate page, from cancer to health insurance, from taking care of your teeth to taking care of your sex life. Of course, it's not thorough on any of these subjects—but it's informative, easy to read, and entertaining.

Popenoe, C. (Ed.), *Wellness*, (A Bibliography of Holistic Health Books), Washington, D.C.: YES! Bookshop, 1978.

Ulene, Art, *Feeling Fine: A 20-Day Program of Pleasures for a Lifetime of Health*. New York: Ballantine Books, 1977.
This is a rather popular book about improving your health with tips on eating, exercising, and dealing with stress, by the doctor on NBC's *Today* show. The book can be used as a wellness program by following its suggestions day by day.

FOR CHAPTER THIRTEEN: "Defusing Hostility"

Layden, Milton, *Escaping the Hostility Trap*. Englewood Cliffs, New Jersey: Prentice-Hall, 1977.
Although this book is somewhat repetitive, it does give plenty of examples and explains clearly the basic theory I've presented in this chapter.

(See also the sources listed with Chapter 14.)

FOR CHAPTER FOURTEEN: "Fear, Depression, and Problem Feelings in General"

Binder, Virginia, Binder, Arnold, and Rimland, Bernard, eds., *Modern Therapies*. Englewood Cliffs, New Jersey: Prentice-Hall, Inc., 1976. This book provides an overview of many major modern therapeutic techniques, with one chapter on each approach (written by a significant practitioner in the field). To learn more about handling problem feelings, see especially the chapters on Rational-Emotive Therapy, Gestalt Therapy, Transcendental Meditation, Implosive Therapy, and Behavior Modification.

Ellis, Albert, and Grieger, Russel, *RET: Handbook of Rational Emotive Therapy*. New York: Springer Publishing Company, Inc., 1977.
The chapters on depression are particularly helpful, notably Aaron Beck and Brian Shaw's "Cognitive Approaches to Depression" and "The Treatment of Depression with Cognitive Therapy."

Marks, Isaac, *Living with Fear*. (Publication data not available.)
This book is a "cognitive behavior therapy" approach to fear. That is, the author suggests ways of thinking ("cognitive") and ways of acting ("behavior") to help you overcome your fears.

Meichenbaum, Donald, ed., *Cognitive Behavior Therapy: A Practitioner's Guide*. New York: BMA Audio Cassette Publications, 1978.
This is a set of six cassette tape recordings. It *is* expensive and intended mainly for professional therapists, but it does contain some of the latest in research and therapeutic suggestions on fear, depression, and a number of behavioral problems.

Perls, Frederick S., *Gestalt Therapy Verbatim*. Lafayette, California: Real People Press, 1969.
This is one of the more widely read works on Gestalt, and since it is mostly verbatim examples of people working through their feelings with the help of "Fritz" Perls (the founder of Gestalt Therapy), it gives you a good idea of how you might use the two-chair technique with yourself.

FOR CHAPTER FIFTEEN: "Overcoming Guilt Feelings"

Punzo, Vincent C., *Reflective Naturalism: An Introduction to Moral Philosophy*. New York: The Macmillan Company, 1969.
Although the author's own biases stand out in this book he nonetheless clearly and succinctly examines the major ethical philosophies that have been proposed through history and in the present. If you want some help in finding out which general principles you think should be the foundation for your ethical behavior, then read this introduction to the study of ethics.

Rand, Ayn, *The Virtue of Selfishness: A New Concept of Egoism*. New York: The New American Library, Inc., 1961, 1964.
I do not share Ayn Rand's conclusions about the basis of ethical action (I believe ethics must go beyond the self rather than be limited by it), but she does present an interesting point of view, and one which is quite popular these days. The ideas she presents are worth thinking about.

Simon, Howe, and Kirschenbaum, *Values Clarification*. (See suggestions for Chapter 6.)
You can use this classic work on values focussing to help clarify your own ethical, or moral values. I particularly suggest the following exercises from the book because they have a bearing on moral decision-making: "Forced Choice Ladder"; "The Values Journal"; "Alternative Action Search"; "Chairs or Dialogue with Self"; "Percentage Questions"; "The Pie of Life"; "Strength of Values"; "Alligator River"; "Self Contracts"; "Ways to Live"; and "Who's to Blame?"

FOR CHAPTER SIXTEEN: "Liking Yourself"

Canfield, Jack, and Wells, Harold C., *100 Ways to Enhance Self-Concept in the Classroom*. Englewood Cliffs, New Jersey: Prentice Hall, Inc., 1976.
Like its predecessor, *Values Clarification* (which is also helpful for increasing self-esteem—see above), this book contains many exercises for helping you realize how neat you are! Although originally written for educators, it has practical value for any adult

who wants to increase liking for self.

Elkins, Dov Peretz, ed., *Glad to Be Me: Building Self-Esteem in Yourself and Others*. Englewood Cliffs, New Jersey: Prentice-Hall, Inc., 1976.
This little book is a collection of thoughtful and inspiring quotations from many sources that can help you affirm yourself and really care about *you*.

Simon, Sidney, *I Am Loveable and Capable: A Modern Allegory on the Classical Put-Down*. Niles, Illinois: Argus Communications, 1973, 1974.
This short story graphically illustrates how we get some of our bad feelings about ourselves and—implicitly—how we can counteract this tendency and shore up our feelings of self-worth.

FOR CHAPTER SEVENTEEN: "Who Are You? (Really)"

Berne, Eric, *Games People Play*. New York: Grove Press, Inc., 1964.
The subject of Berne's book differs from the content of this chapter, but it *is* an interesting supplement—especially if you see people's "acts" as games they play to achieve ulterior motives.

Fenwick, Sheridan, *Getting It: The Psychology of est*. Philadelphia and New York: J.B. Lippincott Company, 1976.
Chapter 6 of Fenwick's book, "Get Off Your Act," ties in with Chapter 17.

FOR CHAPTER EIGHTEEN: "How to Have Your Own Soap Opera"

Berne, Eric, *Games People Play*. (See above.)

Steiner, Claude M., *Scripts People Live*. New York: Grove Press, Inc., 1974.
Both of these books are written by "T.A." (Transactional Analysis) psychologists—the first is by the founder of T.A. (and actually started the T.A. movement). Although neither of these books focuses on soap operas *per se*, both offer interesting descriptions of

the various stories (or scripts) and ritual games that we act out, usually unwittingly. Both books certainly go far beyond the scope of this chapter, and I don't necessarily subscribe to all the ideas they contain—but they do make fascinating supplemental reading.

FOR CHAPTER NINETEEN: "Making Life the Best Possible Game"

This chapter puts together the rest of the book, so the suggestions for further reading are to be found above.

MISCELLANEOUS RESOURCES

James, Muriel, and Jongeward, Dorothy, *Born to Win: Transactional Analysis with Gestalt Experiments*. Reading, Massachusetts; Menlo Park, California; London; and Don Mills, Ontario: Addison-Wesley Publishing Company, 1971.

Smith, Adam, *Powers of Mind*. New York: Ballantine Books, 1975.

ABOUT THE AUTHOR

Dr. Tony Larsen is a part-time teacher and psychological counselor. From his experience and study of various brands of therapy he has put together for his courses and counseling his own combination of guidelines and suggestions for handling your world more effectively. Tony doesn't claim that his methods are unique or original. He just claims that they work.

Tony is also an ordained Unitarian Universalist minister serving a church in Racine, Wisconsin, having received his B.A. from Maryknoll College (majors in psychology and philosophy), his M.A. from Maryknoll School of Theology, and his D.Mn. from Meadville/Lombard Theological School.